MW01076174

Fr. Spitzer's Universe

Also by Fr. Robert Spitzer:

The Four Levels of Happiness

Apologetics I: The Catholic Faith and Science

Fr. Robert Spitzer, S.J., Ph.D.

Fr. Spitzer's

UNIVERSE

Exploring Life's Big Questions

Edited by Dr. Edward H. Chandler

EWTN Publishing, Inc.
Irondale, Alabama

EWTN Publishing, Inc.

5817 Old Leeds Road, Irondale, AL 35210

Distributed by Sophia Institute Press, Box 5284, Manchester, NH 03108.

paperback ISBN 978-1-68278-285-9
ebook ISBN 978-1-68278-286-6

Library of Congress Control Number: 2024944135

First printing

Contents

Publisher's Note

The format of this EWTN Publishing book mimics the question-and-answer style of the EWTN program *Father Spitzer's Universe*. Questions from viewers and listeners are posed to Fr. Spitzer, introduced by host Doug Keck, often with follow-up or explanatory queries. This work is a faithful reproduction of these timely theological questions and answers, edited and approved by Fr. Spitzer.

I Believe in God the Father

Proofs of God's Existence

Give us a foolproof argument for the existence of a Creator. Is there some proof that atheists cannot deny, or one particular argument that you find most effective?

I think one of the most effective arguments comes from Bernard Lonergan in chapter 19 of his book *Insight: A Study of Human Understanding*. Lonergan's proof runs like this: If the real is completely intelligible, then God exists. But the real *is* completely intelligible. Therefore, God exists. I know that is a mouthful with the big word *intelligible*," but let's break it up into four steps which might make it "intelligible." First, we will prove that there must be at least one uncaused reality in the whole of reality. Let's begin with some definitions. A *caused reality* is one that cannot exist without a cause beyond itself. An *uncaused reality* is one that exists through itself and therefore does not need a cause outside of itself to exist. Now if the whole of reality were caused realities, then the whole of reality would itself be a caused reality and would need a cause in order to exist. But if this cause is outside of the whole of reality, then it would not exist, and so the whole of reality (which is dependent on it) would likewise not exist. In this case, the whole of reality would be nothing. But that is clearly not the case: there is something (many things). So, there has to be at least one Reality that is uncaused. This is where we get the traditional notion of an "uncaused Cause." I don't think any atheist can get out of that proof of the existence of at least one uncaused Cause, because if you have an infinity of caused causes—an infinite succession of realities, each of which needs to be caused in order to exist, and which is nothing before it is caused—then they are all nothing in their totality. They can't possibly exist. Again, that is obviously not the case. So, that, in my opinion, is foolproof.

Second, Lonergan shows that an uncaused cause has to be perfectly intelligible. That is to say, an uncaused Cause which exists through itself, and explains existence itself, will have the answer to every possible question that can be asked about existence. Thus, it has to be the ultimate answer to every question that can be posed about existence or reality.

Third, if the uncaused Cause is perfectly intelligible, Lonergan goes on to say, it must be an unrestricted act of understanding. In brief, Lonergan shows that a reality that is completely intelligible (and contains the complete set of correct answers to the complete set of questions within itself) cannot be a material reality or any other finite reality because material and finite realities must pose questions that they themselves cannot answer about existence (the whole of reality), and so must be incomplete. Therefore, the only reality that can be completely intelligible is an immaterial act of understanding which is *unrestricted*. (Lonergan has an extended proof of this in chapter 19.)

Fourth, given that the uncaused Cause is itself an unrestricted act of understanding, it must be one and only one because there can only be one unrestricted reality. A second unrestricted reality would have to be different from the first, but the differentiating factor implies that the second unrestricted reality would have to be in some way restricted (in space-time point activity, power, dimension, etc.), which is an obvious contradiction.

In conclusion, since there must be one uncaused reality, and that reality must be a *unique* unrestricted act of understanding, there must exist a unique uncaused reality that is an unrestricted act of understanding and the ultimate cause of the whole of reality (a Creator). This is what we mean by "God."

This is a very good proof, which I expound in my book, *The Soul's Upward Yearning: Clues to Our Transcendent Nature from Experience and Reason.* I also address this in chapter 4 of my earlier book called *New Proofs for the Existence of God: Contributions of Contemporary Physics and Philosophy.*

A final note: In his book, Lonergan gives a plea to his readers, that if he (Lonergan) has done something wrong, if there is error in this proof, if there is some contradiction that either he or others haven't seen, tell him what it is. Of course, nothing has been forthcoming.

God the Creator — The Universe

How would one best respond to the claim of an eternal universe that goes through cycles of expansion and contraction? What does modern science say about this claim, and how does that relate to our belief in God?

This question refers to what is also called "the bouncing universe theory" or "the oscillating universe theory." We know that our universe in this current expansion is "only" 13.8 billion years old. One of the hypotheses that suggests a universe older than 13.8 billion years posits that the universe is repeatedly expanding from a big bang and contracting into a big crunch: "exploding," then expanding and eventually contracting, only to repeat the cycle. Supposedly it has been doing this forever.

Now, there are many different reasons why you can't have an eternally bouncing universe. We'll address two of them. First, there is the problem that each cycle has to get bigger, and if so, it must be the case that a given cycle has only been around for a finite amount of time. If you were to go backwards in time, you would not be able to go backwards infinitely; you would go backwards to a particular point in the finite past.

The second reason comes from dark energy itself. According to the standard cosmological model, the universe is made up of three major groups of what we might call "mass-energy." There is visible matter, which constitutes 5 percent of the universe; dark matter, which accounts for roughly 25 percent; and then there is dark energy, which causes the universe to accelerate in its expansion, which is 70 percent of the mass energy in the universe. It is worth repeating: dark energy makes the universe accelerate in its expansion. That means that if the preponderance of dark energy were always part of the universe, then the universe could not possibly have collapsed in upon itself in any past era. The only way you could get it to collapse upon itself is to get rid of the dark energy and then suddenly in the next cycle reintroduce it. Thus, in an oscillating universe, God comes into the world just to fool us, taking out the dark energy, letting the universe collapse, and then putting it back in. As if He says, "Fooled you!" But, it is highly unlikely that God is playing games.

In view of the above two arguments, it is highly likely that the universe is finite in past time, implying a Creator outside of the universe as its origin.

Listening to all of this higher theory with its apparent complications, the average person might ask, "Why didn't God make the universe much simpler? Why did God choose to do it this way?"

All these technical terms do seem to imply that the universe is very complicated. No doubt there are complexities in it; but the most amazing thing about the universe itself is that it is remarkably simple in its underpinnings. For example, the various physical constants, such as the speed of light in a vacuum, and the interaction of very fundamental equations that bring together practically everything with an astonishing elegance and beauty, attest to the universe's intelligibility and its remarkable simplicity. Study of these things demonstrates that the hand of God is incredibly elegant.

Another example of this elegance is found in our method of doing physics. In particle physics and other areas of physics, we look for the most elegant solution for our theory, and then build our experimental apparatus to find it. Astonishingly, more often than not, there it is! This manifests a highly improbable mathematical, physical, and aesthetic elegance. I don't believe for a second that such elegance happened to occur by pure chance. The universe is mathematical from its top to its bottom, but it is not *merely* mathematical. It is elegantly mathematical. It is linearly and nonlinearly mathematical, and this elegance makes its complexity into a simple unity—incredibly harmonious and beautiful.

All of that comes together in this most remarkable way that speaks not only of intelligence, but also of God's love, because He did this for humankind. God did this to bring life, and not just mere life but life to the fullest, with intelligence, that would go on to support a spirit, a soul that produces a unique manifestation of self-consciousness united with this created beauty that would look back in stunned wonder.

Like the Holy Scripture says: we are "fearfully and wonderfully made";[1] and "the heavens are telling the glory of God."[2] We look

---

[1] Ps. 139:14, NRSVCE.
[2] Ps. 19:1.

back upon this mathematical, physical, and aesthetic elegance and are awed by the fact that we have been loved into existence.

How do I explain an expanding universe in relationship to God?

That is a good physics question. Yes, the universe is expanding; as a matter of fact, its expansion is accelerating. In relation to God, I would say that God is "thinking" the universe bigger. God can conceive of anything, whether temporal or spatial. He can think of me and you and of the whole universe simultaneously. So, of course, He can think it bigger and bigger. In other words, God, in His unrestricted act of thinking and of loving, wills the universe to expand, and so it inevitably gets bigger and bigger. For all intents and purposes, God's thoughts do not delimit Him. If He thinks of a thought that is temporal or spatial, it does not limit Him in His nature any more than my thinking of a balloon expanding in my mind right now turns me into a balloon. I'm basically still me thinking, and the balloon is just a thought that I'm thinking about, and of course, it is the same thing with God.

God the Creator—Creation and Science

Is the story of creation scientifically accurate? Sure, God could create all the animals in one day if He wanted to, but did He? And, if it is not scientifically accurate, is there harm in believing it?

Pope Pius XII answered that for us in his two encyclicals: *Divino Afflante Spiritu* (1943) and *Humani Generis* (1950). You can easily get these encyclicals online, and there are a number of good interpretations of them. I will give the gist of them. In *Divino Afflante Spiritu*, Pope Pius XII says that the purpose of the Bible and of its Creation story is to give us sacred truths necessary for salvation.

It is not meant to give us a scientifically precise description and explanation of the physical universe and its physical operations. In other words, the motive in writing the Creation story is other than doing science. It is the job of science and the scientific method, the pope says, to give a physically accurate description and explanation of the physical universe. So, in answer to your question, does the Bible give a scientifically accurate picture of Creation? No, it does not. Again, why? Because its purpose was not to give a scientific explanation of Creation; its purpose is to give sacred truths necessary for salvation.

Understanding the context of the Creation narrative helps us see what Pope Pius XII is saying. Ancient Israel, God's Old Testament people, had a big problem: they were surrounded by various cultures that were influencing their own culture and belief. We can see this not only in the Bible itself, but also in those cultures' own epic creation stories that we still have. An obvious falsehood shared by all these epics is that there are innumerable "gods": the sea is a god, the stars are gods, the sun is a god. The cultures surrounding ancient Israel essentially believed that many natural things are gods. But in truth there is only one God. So, of course, our author has to counter and correct that belief, which was infecting the belief of the Israelites. No, there are not many gods; there is but one God. All these things that the world believes to be gods are no gods at all; they and everything else are creations of God. There is no ocean god; the ocean is a creation of God. There is no star god or moon god; the moon and the stars are all creations of the one God.

Then, you have another terrible distortion in the rival myths to Israel: that human beings are just cannon fodder, playthings for the gods, created as slaves to relieve the gods of labor. We're the pawns in a cosmic game. The author of Genesis says, *No! It is not like that at all. You are actually created in the image and likeness of God Himself.* Once God had finished creating, according to Genesis 1, He looked at all that He had made and said, "It is very good." God created nothing evil. So, a major purpose of the author of Genesis is to reconfigure all of these epic creation stories in a way that communicates Truth—the sacred truths necessary for salvation.

Consider these four things alone: one God, Who created all things, Who made humankind in His own image, and Who made it all very good. This is critically important for salvation. On the other hand, if you ask for a scientifically accurate picture of Creation, our understanding in the scientific world is that the universe is approximately 13.8 billion years old; that the mass of visible matter in the universe is roughly 10^{55} kilograms; that there is five times more dark matter by mass than visible matter; and that there is almost three times more dark energy than there is dark matter. In other words, it is about 70 percent dark energy, 25 percent dark matter, and 5 percent visible matter.

In addition, we know that our physical universe evolved in a certain way. We can actually detail that precisely. God created the entire universe in a quantum cosmological moment, where space, time, gravity, and the other three cosmological forces—the strong nuclear force, the weak nuclear force, and the electromagnetic force—were all combined into one unified field that "exploded" and literally gave rise to the entire material universe. It did this so symmetrically and elegantly that it just began to unfold into the orderly cosmos we see today.

As you look at the Genesis 1 Creation narrative from the perspective of science, you see remarkable parallels. For example, "Let there be light!"—the first day of Creation.[3] How did the author

---

[3] Gen. 1:3.

of Genesis know that? That is scientifically very accurate. And how does he know how this unraveling occurs, for there are all kinds of parallels between the scientific account and the Genesis account. I don't have the space to detail all those parallels for you here, but the answer to the question "How did he know?" is that God revealed it to him, of course, but not in scientific language.

In essence, Pope Pius XII is telling us in *Divino Afflante Spiritu*, let the Bible be the Bible for sacred truths and let science be science to strive for accurate physical descriptions and explanations. The two are perfectly compatible because they are talking about two completely different spheres of understanding. Science can't replace theology—and theology doesn't replace science. Both sources of knowledge come from the same ultimate source, namely God. Faith and reason are completely compatible. There is no danger in accepting the scientific account of Creation; you are free to believe that account. You are also free to believe in the biblical account and the message of salvation we need to hear that tells us about the one God, about what nature really is and the goodness of the material world around us, and about the true dignity and destiny of humanity.

We are supposed to believe that all that the Catholic Church declares is revealed by God. How do we reconcile this when it seems that the Church didn't accept Galileo's teachings on the universe, only coming around to accepting them much later? A second question is besides pride, for example, why do you think Galileo double-crossed the pope and went public with his views?

Honestly, it is a complete mystery, not only to me but also to a lot of historians, why Galileo behaved as he did: why he insulted his friend, Pope Urban VIII, and alienated his friends at the Jesuit college. Ego seems to be the only explanation. Galileo didn't want to be silenced. The issue wasn't about the heliocentric solar system. The Church had already accepted the possibility of that. They were just waiting for observational evidence, which didn't come until two centuries later in 1832 when the German astronomer Friedrich Bessel measured the first accurate stellar parallax, proving the heliocentric solar system. That is all the Church asked Galileo to do. She wasn't opposed to the heliocentric solar system. The Church wanted proof just like any peer-reviewed scientific journal would want the proof if some author were trying to publish his own claimed discovery. Whether the solar system is heliocentric or not is a factual claim, and you have to back up claims of fact with observational evidence. Galileo didn't do that. That was the Church's big concern—that Galileo didn't have the evidence.

[Doug:] Here is a good question that dovetails well with what you've said so far. Where was Galileo coming from when he stated it flatly in public? Perhaps it wasn't just the issue of theory; rather, there seemed to be an attack by him on the teachings of the Church or how the Bible was to be interpreted. So our questioner asks: Can you address the theory that Galileo was an atheist?

Galileo was not an atheist. Indeed, he had a very credible religious belief as a devout lifelong Catholic, though he may have had his disagreements with how the Bible was to be interpreted. Nevertheless, he still carried on very fine relationships with people in the Church, even after his "exile," which was a comfortable one.

[Doug:] Whether it [biblical interpretation] had been an overly literalistic approach or in which ways things could be taken specifically or how the people of their time would have understood what was being said and what was meant.

Back in 1943, Pope Pius XII laid down those rules of interpretation. He basically said, "Look, there are two views of inspiration." You have the dictation view, where God would, in essence, come to the biblical author and have him take down exactly what He says, with no participation in the construction of the text by the biblical author himself. Though there are some schools of Christian thought that do hold that view, we as Catholics do not. We hold a participatory view of biblical inspiration, which means that the biblical author had a part to play in the construction of the text. As he writes under the inspiration of the Holy Spirit, he is going to be using categories that come from his own culture and from his own intellectual formation. He will not use a mathematical conceptualization of the physical universe because they didn't know anything about that in 500 B.C. As explained above, the Bible was written to convey sacred truths needed for salvation.

Man

Evidence for the Soul

[Doug:] Father, regarding evidence for the soul, earlier in the show you indicated that you wanted to talk a little bit more. Can you give us an overview of this point?

There are six kinds of evidence for the soul. Some of these kinds of evidence go back to ancient times, especially to Plato and St. Augustine, and are developed in the Middle Ages by, for example, Thomas Aquinas. However, many of them are quite contemporary. Here I intend only to survey the different kinds of evidence. Next week, we can talk about them in detail and maybe even get questions about them.

First is the linguistic anthropological evidence of the soul. This is based on the work of two authors, Noam Chomsky and Robert Berwick, in their book entitled *Why Only Us*. They consider what happened seventy thousand years ago that gave rise to human beings having a universal syntactical linguistic revolution that led to the multiplicity of languages and to universal grammar and syntax. Chomsky and Berwick make no argument for the soul; in fact, they look for a naturalistic explanation, whereas transcendental philsophers insist that only a transphysical soul accounts for the emergence of such a linguistic revolution, along with the capacity for abstraction evident in burial of the dead, artistic and symbolic representations on the walls of caves, mathematical proclivity, and social norms. Chomsky and Berwick admit that they have not found a naturalistic explanation and that the answer may not lie in physical processes and structures. In view of this, they recommend looking at *philosophical* explanations coming from philosophers of the early modern scientific revolution and the contemporary era. Curiously, these philosophical arguments make recourse to a transphysical soul. We call this argument the "linguistic anthropological argument."

Second are near-death experiences, specifically such experiences documented in good longitudinal studies published in good peer-reviewed medical journals. There are so many of these studies that the New York Academy of Sciences affirmed the credible possibility of your consciousness surviving bodily death. What evidence makes this conclusion so probative? First, there is considerable evidence of clinically dead people (flat EEG, fixed and dilated pupils, and no gag reflex) accurately reporting data taking place outside the operating room and even outside the hospital. Furthermore, 80 percent of blind people see (most of them for the first time) when they are clinically dead. Additionally, many clinically dead people report going over to the other side and getting previously unknown information from relatives.

Third are the five transcendental desires: for perfect truth, love, goodness, fairness, perfect beauty, and a perfect home. Those five transcendental desires portray an awareness of things that we never could have gotten from the natural, observable world or from a "rewiring" of our brain. In other words, the awareness of perfect truth is beyond any physical process and beyond anything that we can experience in the world. The awareness of perfect love is beyond the physical processes of our brains and the natural, observable world. The same can be said about the awareness of perfect fairness, beauty, and home.

Fourth, there is a difference between what we call "syntactical language" and a mere perceptual idea. For example, chimpanzees can be taught 150 signs of American Sign Language. All of those signs by themselves represent perceptual ideas, like *dog*, *cat*, and *man*. However, with all of that sign recognition, no chimpanzee can distinguish between "dog bites man" and "man bites dog" because they cannot distinguish a subject from a predicate or a subject from an object. Why not? Because they don't have *con*ceptual ideas; they only have *per*ceptual ideas—they do not have a power of abstraction enabling them to understand relationships, groups, and all other non-individuated ideas. As Aquinas and many modern philosophers show, the power of abstraction requires high-level abstract ideas to form the groups and categories needed for the abstraction process itself. But the innate presence of these high-level ideas cannot be reduced to physical processes and structures precisely because they are immaterial abstractions. Hence, human conceptual ideas require something transphysical—something immaterial—like a soul.

Then we get into a fifth area: mathematics, especially the work of Kurt Gödel, who actually developed a proof showing that the way human beings understand mathematics must be transalgorithmic. It can't be based on a set of programs or rules that are pre-programmed into a human mind. Mathematical reasoning is always transcending the previous set of algorithms, programs, and rules. So, human beings transcend particular mathematical expressions, showing that our thought is not reducible to physical and algorithmically finite processes and structures. But only an immaterial power—like a soul—can be beyond physically and algorithmically finite processes and structures. This is what differentiates human beings from computers. Computers can never go beyond the rules, forms, and processes they have been given, whereas human mathematicians do this all the time. Apparently, computers don't have souls.

Then, you go to a sixth, equally fascinating area, as formulated by New York University philosopher David J. Chalmers as the Hard Problem of Consciousness. This deals with the fact that "the inwardness of Human subjectivity" cannot be explained by a physical process. Other arguments have articulated the same problem in a slightly different way. Chalmers talks about our "experiencing of our experiencing." This is what gives rise to the inwardness of subjectivity. If you experience yourself experiencing or are aware of yourself being aware, you must be in two relative positions with respect to yourself at the same time, and no physical process, not even a quantum process, can do this. Some distinguished physicists and biologists have tried to explain this, but in my opinion, it is impossible to explain the experience of experiencing and awareness of being aware by means of a physical process alone, since it can't come from the outward experience itself. There is something transcendental, something like a soul, that imparts to humans this ability.

In sum, when you put all these kinds of evidence together, they form a strong comprehensive complementary foundation for a transphysical soul in human beings. In view of this, you almost have to be willfully blind to deny the transphysical, transmaterial soul because the evidence for it is so overwhelming.

So, what is going on with the materialists' denial of a soul? The problem is not a lack of evidence. The evidence is out there to see for anyone who is at least remotely open and willing to be instructed. The problem is that the materialists don't want to believe in transcendence, because transcendence implies a God to Whom they might be responsible. Or, they don't want to believe in transcendence because they only want to believe in what they can see. That arbitrary denial of our transcendent capacity is like giving yourself a frontal lobotomy because you don't like the implications of being intelligent. My point is, this is not rationally motivated because it turns a blind eye to so much evidence—particularly the studies of near-death experiences. As you are going to see in the next week when we start explaining some of these remarkable data, religion makes a lot of sense. And when we add to it that the soul is the vehicle through which God communicates to human beings, through the numinous experience, we'll find that there is also good evidence for the immortality of the soul. This is just a little *précis* of what we're going to discuss next week.

Was that chimpanzee named after the philosopher?

Yes. Nim Chimpsky was named after Noam Chomsky, who has for a long time been at the forefront of linguistics and the philosophy of language. Scholars like Herbert Terrace have tested Chomsky's controversial claim that only humans have language. Terrace studied the primate class, and claimed to have demonstrated that no chimpanzee could ever pass Chomsky's syntax test. For example, it could never discern the difference between "dog bites man" and "man bites dog." A chimpanzee can appropriate many signs in American Sign Language; it can learn the signs for *man, dog, bite,* and so forth, even up to 150 signs. But it can't understand the syntactical significance of those words in a sentence, something that every two-year-old child understands. So, we can say that "ape language" is in no way analogous to human language.

We make a distinction that says that, like human beings, apes have *perceptions,* but only human beings have *concepts,* which involve relationships among ideas. Concepts include predicates, direct objects, indirect objects, logical and mathematical relationships, and prepostitional phrases, among many other abstractions that enable humans to relate ideas to each other and to the questions where, when, how, what, and why. No chimpanzee has this ability. The only way you can form concepts (abstract relationships independent of individual objects) is through a power that transcends physical processes and structures—like a soul. There is very good proof of this in St. Thomas Aquinas's *Summa Theologica*, First Part, question 79. Bernard Lonergan also addresses this in a chapter on the notion of being in his book *Insight*.

The Fall

The Problem of Evil

God is all-knowing; He knew that His angel of light would be consumed with pride and turned into the devil. Why did He then go ahead and create him?

This is a very good question. God wanted in His generosity to create free creatures, creatures that "move" inside themselves, away from the light, or outside of themselves, into the light. That is, God created a creature and let that creature, as it were, make the decisions that would form its essence. So, He created a "Lucifer," or *light bearer*, who was as the name indicates. He was perhaps the highest of all angels. Despite all this, in his freedom he became consumed with pride and really thought that he was the be-all and the end-all. When he took that option to turn inward, to evil, God didn't destroy him; rather, God literally said that if that is the way you want to live, that is the way you shall indeed live. As a result, he is banished from God and from His kingdom. And Lucifer, the devil, now Satan "the accuser," even though he is in darkness, emptiness, alienation, and pain, still has his one little glimmer of perverse "happiness": the fact that he can cause in others the same darkness, alienation, and pain of being separated from God and from His blessing, by tempting them to turn to the same darkness that envelops him.

You might be thinking, could somebody persistently continue to want to do that? Satan definitively wants for all time to be in the darkness rather than in the light, to be in his own little minimal world of self-worship and egocentricity rather than the great light-filled and loving Kingdom of God. Every single one of us has essentially the same choice. Like Satan, we can actually choose to be in a tiny, alienating, empty, lonely world. But even there, I've got something that I can hold on to: egocentricity, domination of others, and of course, self-worship. I can have those three things in my life if I want them. But if I choose them, then I've also chosen isolation from God filled with emptiness, darkness, loneliness, devoid of love and companionship.

God does not destroy us for so doing. If God were to destroy everyone who is going to make that decision, if He chose not to create them because of their decision, then His creatures have no genuine free will and thus no real dignity. Thus, He has to let some creatures err.

[Doug:] Otherwise, in a sense, we'd be like humanoids—robots—who do the right thing but with no control and no real will, because we're not in a position to choose. But let me follow up on something you said. You mentioned a little glimmer of perverse happiness that the devil or the demons get when they tempt us. Is that because of what they do to us? Or because they are getting back at God? Or both?

Absolutely both. In German it is called *schadenfreude*: pleasure in another person's pain, the happiness of darkness from undermining love, the happiness that comes from undermining the One Who created us in love, a pure assertion of ego over the Creator Himself. Again, if that is what you want to do, God is going to allow you to do that. But in the end, that perverse happiness, filled with darkness, alienation, and loneliness will not make you happy. Our only true and ultimate happiness resides in God alone, Who is perfect Love, Truth, Beauty, and Goodness.

What Satan and his demons want is to deceive us into the false and dark perverse happiness. Deceive us into *schadenfreude*. If you hadn't had that awesome freedom to choose perverse and deceitful happiness, then your love for God would never be your own, because you never really had a choice to begin with. You would be just programmed to do one thing, loving behaviors. The love didn't originate from you at all, but rather originates from your "programming." But God wanted to create us in His own image and likeness, with wills free to really choose Him.

If God loves us so much, why did He cast Satan and his league of angels down to earth, to surround us with all the evil that exists in the world today? It is overwhelming.

You can actually defeat evil—even on a grand, angelic scale by your cooperation with the Good! You—and every human being—have been called to this dignity. And not just to the struggle on the earth, but to the struggle in Heaven as well, as Ephesians 6:12 indicates.[4] God has allowed us to be involved in a heavenly struggle, one that He will ultimately win, and one in which we have an important part to play.

J. R. R. Tolkein, a Catholic genius, in his *Lord of the Rings* trilogy, gives to the little Hobbit Frodo the task of carrying the ring of power to volcanic Mount Doom, where he is to cast the ring into the magma. Now you could say, well, that is just fiction, but it bears comparison to our calling. None of us is called to do what Frodo did. Jesus has already defeated evil; He has, as it were, thrown

---

[4] "For we are not contending against flesh and blood, but against the principalities, against the powers, against the world rulers of this present darkness, against the spiritual hosts of wickedness in the heavenly places."

the ring into Mount Doom. But Frodo's achievement was not the end of the story. There were still battles to fight. In a similar way, we can play an incredibly important part in the ongoing, though already-won, cosmic struggle. It is a dignity we've been given in our lifetimes to be allowed to participate. We have a big part to play, but it does, as the questioner implied, involve temptations and struggles.

If you are feeling overwhelmed, try to understand what is causing such a feeling: Too much media or news? Whatever it is, take it to prayer. Go talk to a priest; go to the Sacrament of Reconciliation; go to Eucharistic adoration, by which you can better center yourself so that you will not feel so overwhelmed. And of course, remember the importance of the Eucharist as your protection against evil. Remember also the prayers to St. Michael, to Mary, and to the Lord Jesus, Whose name is powerful. These things, too, can mitigate the feelings of being overwhelmed.

The Effects of the Fall

I never knew Adam and Eve. Why should I be punished for their sins? Isn't this cruel and unfair?

You are right in your insight. We are not accountable for Adam and Eve. But it is not that we're being punished for what they did; we are suffering a consequence for what they did. When you say "punished," you imply some retributive intent on the part of God. There is no retributive intent on God's part, but there is a consequence: for Adam and Eve it is Original Sin, and that consequence does hit us.

Let me try to explain this more fully. The first man and woman, Adam and Eve, are each given a soul. They have, of course, all of the biological features of male and female human beings, but the one thing that differentiates them from every other animal—this is stated very clearly in Pope Pius XII's encyclical, *Humani Generis*—is the presence in each of them of a transphysical soul. In the foregoing pages, we have seen considerable significant evidence of this soul from medical studies of near-death experiences and terminal lucidity, studies of uniquely human linguistics, the capacity for creative mathematics, our transcendental desires, religious experience, and other capacities. Our capacity to survive bodily death was given to us from the very beginning; it is truly what makes us in the image and likeness of God.[5] Because we have souls with intellect and will, we have free will; we have the capacity for moral reflection. We have the capacity to know God, something that no higher primate has, much less lower animals.

So, we possess this soul, and in it, we have abstract understanding and moral reflection, and through this soul we're able to be aware of God. Through this soul we're able to do abstract thinking, even mathematical thinking. In this soul, we're given the capacity to do so many other things that primates will never be able to do. For example, they have no art; they have no sense of transcendence whatsoever. They have no self-consciousness. A dog can get sad when the master leaves the home, but it doesn't reflect back upon itself and say, "Gosh, I am sad!" and become depressed because it recognizes its sadness. The dog is just sad. Then the master comes back and the dog wags its tail, because it's happy to see the master. But unlike the dog, we reflect on our mood and on our thoughts. These things have been put together in us elegantly by the Lord.

One thing in particular is going to result from human self-consciousness applied to moral reasoning, to abstractions, and to

---

[5] Gen. 1:26.

the awareness of God: freedom of the will. Yet, we are also aware of one other thing: that "Lucifer," the prince of the evil beings, was right there with Adam and Eve immediately after their creation. He intends to insert himself into the human condition. He can never take over the souls of Adam and Eve, nor can he force them to do anything that they don't want to do. So, he must act through their free will. He approaches the first man and woman, and the first thing he says is, "Hey. There is one thing you can't have. Why do you think that God wants to deprive you of this? Is He holding back something from you?" From the beginning the devil seeks in the minds of Adam and Eve to pit egocentricity against the gift of love.

At some juncture he puts the question (and answer) to them (he does it deceptively and assiduously, and is still at it, constantly): "Don't you really want to take this forbidden fruit? Of course you really *do* because you are going to be like a god!" Adam and Eve are provoked to thinking, "Wow—godlike wisdom would be pretty good. I think I would like to be God instead of letting God be God." But the minute they act on this, kaboom! A terrible thing happens—they sense the loss of communion with God. Before the Fall, God's presence to Adam and Eve was intimate and powerful; they knew His goodness; they knew His presence in a way that we do not. At the moment of their sin, the moment they misused their freedom and chose to set God to the side, to try to become like gods themselves—the very sin that the devil himself committed—they ruined for themselves the very gifts that God had given them, including the sense of His presence.

Here is the thing to remember: we are going to inherit, as it were, that same *loss* of the deep sense of God's presence and His goodness. But we're not Calvinists: we do not believe that we lost that sense of God's deep goodness and presence completely. The

Catholic Church has always held that, although fallen and corrupted, human beings are still essentially good. In fact, I think there is a lot of evidence for that. I think we do still have a profound awareness of God's presence, although it is, as St. Paul says, as if looking through a glass darkly.[6] We don't get that full impact. Because we have been impacted by Adam, we suffer a significant, but not total, inability to be aware of the profundity of God's presence. It is as if Adam introduced into our souls that darkened glass. This is transmitted from generation to generation, but *not* as something punitive. Rather, it is something that is a natural consequence of the misuse of freedom. Are we still free? Yes. Are we still aware of God's presence in our lives? Yes. Are we aware of God's presence sufficiently to be able to do good works and, by our free will, to choose God? Absolutely, and all the more so in light of the redemption of Christ, because now we have the power of the Holy Spirit.

If we're taking the Fall story literally, could Eve have sinned on her own? Did she have to convince her husband to eat the fruit? Was it something they had to cooperate in doing, or could she have committed the Original Sin on her own?

In my opinion, the very minute she commits the Original Sin, she is "looking through a glass darkly." She feels the effect of her loss, and so what does she want to do? Misery loves company! She wants to share the loss with her husband. She wants to mitigate her loss by bringing Adam into the sin. But he freely, willingly says, "Yeah, sounds good," and of course, because he does that by his own act of freedom, he is co-involved from the very beginning.

---

[6] 1 Cor. 13:12.

But yeah, she could have technically commited the Original Sin without co-opting Adam.

[Doug:]But that is not how the story goes. One other question, though. If I am born 51 percent good, then is it possible for me to continue to be good without God's help?

Without God's help? No, because the 51 percent good that you have is already *with* God's help. The "51 percent good" means that God is already present to you. So, you are already living in grace. The *complete* corruption of human nature would indicate that God had just simply withdrawn. If that were true, Calvin would be right; your nature would be completely corrupted.

Corruption of the will occurs to the extent that God withdraws. But God doesn't "withdraw" from us in that Calvinistic sense at all. The Catholic Church teaches that God still remains present to human consciousness but that Adam chose to put on those dark glasses, which mitigate the full effects of God's presence to human consciousness. So, it is not that God is withdrawing; it is that we inherit "the glass darkly," which of course is dulling our consciousness of God's presence. But grace is always present and God is always present to every human consciousness. Human will has not fallen, but it does have what is called *concupiscence*, which is the tendency toward sin, because the human cannot fully discern and appropriate the effects of God's presence as Adam and Eve could, prior to their first sin.

If God creates each individual soul at conception, how can Original Sin be inherited to corrupt our soul? Is it only our flesh that inherits sin?

The soul itself is actually inhibited by the condition into which it is incarnated, if I may put it that way. In other words, God creates this soul. It is a self-reflective soul. But the soul had the vision of God at one time in a very pristine sense. So, it is not just the body but the soul actually has this vision, which is a gift of God. The vision of God is not a property that belongs to the soul in itself. So, essentially, the soul has this sense of itself. It has all of the faculties we've talked about: self-consciousness, the desire for perfect love, beauty, truth, goodness, and for home. It has that ability to arrive at concepts and has linguistic and syntactical faculties. What it doesn't have is the pure vision of God. That is the gift of God. And we believe that the original Adam and Eve, the couple that got the first self-reflective intellectual souls with those desires for perfect truth, love, goodness, beauty, and home, which include consciousness and an awareness and desire for goodness, God gave those souls a sense of Himself that was almost transparent and pristine, what we call a "paradise state." Though the vision was clear, God did not create them with such a pristine vision that they couldn't take their eyes off of Him. He also gave them free will, and it is free will that gives them the ability to put their eyes on themselves, exclusively.

Genesis 3 describes the sin in this way: first, the devil comes along and tells this soul that God has withheld something from it. "You have all of these other things, and you even see Him. But He has withheld the knowledge of good and evil. He is not giving you something you deserve and that you want." So, as we know, the sin is committed, and when that happens, God, as it were, darkens their vision of Him. This gives rise to a real difficulty. The consequences of their sin make their lives and the choice to act according to their conscience more difficult. God, in effect, says to them, "Okay. If you want this vision of yourself more than you want me, then know this: your life is going to be a tough go." So, God, as it were, darkens their vision of Him. But we're not

Calvinists, we're Catholics. We don't say He darkens their vision of Him completely.

Where, then, are human beings left without the vision of God?

We are left without that natural sense of desiring Him. So, in His goodness, He gives it to us partially. My professor, of happy memory, Fr. Gerald Steckler, used to say, "God created all of us, our souls with 51 percent goodness. With 51 percent ability to see Him as He is! And to see His law as it is." So, there is at least 51 percent of our nature that is oriented toward the [G]ood, toward God, toward His love, and toward His truth. At least 51 percent. We're not totally corrupted. But the vision has been darkened, and we are affected by concupiscence, which is our tendency toward sin, and that makes life much more difficult for us. Now, Jesus Christ has come and has given us His Holy Spirit, from Whom we receive the grace that brings us to the point where, once we have been baptized and freely cooperate with that baptismal grace, we become apostles of Truth, Love, and Goodness. This supernatural grace helps us overcome the darkening that has occurred because of Original Sin and concupiscence.

God's Love and Wrath

In the Old Testament, God doesn't seem very loving, but rather angry when ordering the destruction of various cities. This anger seems to turn into love in the New Testament when we see God as loving father to Christ, His Son. Can you explain this?

Yes, in the Old Testament, there is no doubt that there are passages where God is portrayed as angry, and that means emotionally angry, passionately involved with His people. That portrayal has to be put into the context of certain passages in Exodus where we find the idea that God's anger is oriented towards His mercy. Nevertheless, the anger is there. And you're correct in noting that, in the New Testament, such an emotional display is very limited. In fact, Jesus never really refers to it directly at all. There are certain passages in the New Testament where people think, well, Jesus must have been implying God's anger. But in point of fact, those can easily be explained.

There are four passages that are mistakenly taken as indicating an "angry God." Paul, for example, in Romans 1:18 writes of "the wrath of God," but that is a highly specialized term. "The wrath of God" refers to the judgment under which human beings should have been judged; in other words, a negative judgment that we should receive because of our actions. According to St. Paul, Jesus saves us from the wrath of God, from this negative judgment. Now, how do you know what he means by "the wrath of God" that we deserve and from which Jesus saved us? Think about it: Can you imagine God having to send His own Son into the world to save us from His own emotional outburst? Obviously, Jesus came for more than saving us from God's emotional outburst and anger. He is here to save us from the just deserts that we would deserve under the judgment of our own actions. Jesus is going to replace that just judgment with the unconditional mercy of God.

A second passage that people frequently confuse for God's anger is Jesus' "Seven Woes" of Matthew 23, a severe warning given to the Pharisees. What is going on here? Is Jesus ticked off and having an emotional outburst? No, Jesus is giving a forceful prophetic warning to the Pharisees and scribes, because every time He had tried to confront them in the usual way—with a scriptural argument or something of that nature—they didn't want to listen. So, finally Jesus laid it on them, and He did this by stressing that it was God's concern for their salvation that was driving His passionate confrontation of them; that their idea of God's mercy was so limited compared to what God's real mercy is like that they were destroying themselves and the possibility of their own salvation, in addition to being a stumbling block for others. So, Jesus is giving them a very passionate, prophetic warning, a passion that seems like anger because Jesus used Old Testament prophetic terms that we're not accustomed to: "whitewashed tombs," "full of dead men's bones." In our day, we don't have prophets going around speaking in this way, giving that Jeremiahesque prophetic warning. Jesus finally resorts to that in order to penetrate the Pharisees' thickness and self-righteousness so they will both save themselves and stop turning other poor, contrite sinners away from the Kingdom of God.

The third passage is a Gospel story that is frequently appealed to as emblematic of God's anger: when Jesus goes into the Temple and tips over the money changers' tables and drives them out of the Temple. At first glance some are inclined to see it as Jesus having a really angry moment. But if we think about it for one minute, we are reminded that Jesus has already been to the Temple dozens of times without behaving this way. But all of a sudden, this one day right before His Passion it seems like He is getting really angry. What is that all about? First let us say what it is not about: getting angry. Again, it is prophetic, specifically a prophetic judgment on the Temple administration. Tipping over the tables is not a temper tantrum; rather, it is an act of great symbolic significance. The Temple administration had been very corrupt; they had been concerned with managing money, but they had not been in charge of the spiritual lives of the people. By His action, Jesus is demonstrating that such a regime is going to end, ultimately by throwing them out of the Temple precinct. It means already, of course, that they are going to lose their jobs. But Jesus goes even further: He renders judgment on the Temple, predicts its destruction, and says that it is going to be rebuilt upon a cornerstone—namely Himself—that the builders will have rejected. It will become the new cornerstone of the Church; Jesus will become the new, greater Temple.

So, in point of fact, Jesus is not an angry Son of God, and God is never portrayed as angry by Jesus, and the wrath of God that Jesus saves us from is not an emotional outburst. Though there is some apparent discontinuity with the Old Testament because there are times in the Old Testament when God is portrayed as angry, but even this has to be mitigated by passages from Exodus that show that His anger is to be understood with respect to His just judgment.

The idea that God is punitive is admittedly there in the Old Testament. For example, it says in Exodus 20:5 and Deuteronomy 5:9 that God punishes not only the sinner but also the children of the sinner down to the third and fourth generations. These kinds of retributions are there in the Old Testament, but are simply not present in the New. In fact, in some of the Old Testament prophets, there is already a tendency to move away from retribution. But Jesus replaces that retribution with the Parable of the Prodigal Son, which is an image of unconditional mercy. Jesus is making a definitive transformation. It is in continuity with the Old Testament, but there are certain things that Jesus just drops: the terrifying God, the angry God, the retributive God, the disgusted God, and the Stoic God. Now you have the Father of the Prodigal Son …

[Doug:] … besides the fact that a Pharisee had such a negative view and was often hypocritical. It explains why some of those people would have been so startled by Jesus' approach, because it was so different from what they thought it ought to be.

Without question because there are discontinuities. When you look at the image of God that Jesus portrays, you can imagine what the poor Pharisees were thinking: "Hey, wait a minute! I thought we were doing the right thing by, among other things, excluding people from the Kingdom." Many Pharisees believed that they had been good teachers of the Law, and so they were very surprised at the image of God that Jesus was portraying. But when He preaches that God is the father of the Prodigal Son, and teaches His disciples to address God as "Abba," which means "Daddy," you can see the Pharisees saying, "What?! The Master of the universe, the Infinite One is 'Daddy'? Are you kidding me?" But a lot of Pharisees were convinced to become Christians. We know that there was influence on the Gospel of Matthew from Pharisees who became Christians. Some of the Pharisees rejected Christianity, and eventually the rabbis threw the Christians out of the synagogue, and, of course, that leads to the banishment and diaspora of the Christians.

Love one another regardless of what they have done. I think this teaching alone was a huge shock to the world.

You are absolutely correct. It was part of Jesus' definition of love, His elevation of love, as the highest commandment. And in fact, in the New Testament, no virtue is mentioned more often with respect to love than forgiveness. Why is that the case? Because we cannot proceed without some forgiveness. Violence begets violence, and vengeance begets vengeance. If you don't interrupt that cycle, the violence gets worse and the payback gets worse, and so the cycle becomes incredibly destructive. In contrast, Jesus says that following the heart of His Father, the father of the Prodigal Son, stops that cycle. Jesus puts no limits on it. When He tells Peter to forgive his brother seventy times seven times—seven, which is a prime number, times ten, times seven again, which is another prime number—that is like saying that we should simply forgive an unlimited number of times. There are no conditions.

As for the second part of the question: Is this a shock? Yes, because it is distinct from what came before. Jesus says it outright in Matthew's Gospel: "You have heard that it was said, 'An eye for an eye and a tooth for a tooth' "—this is the *lex talionis*; the law of just retribution—"but I say to you," says Jesus, "do not resist one who is evil. But if any one strikes you on the right cheek, turn to him the other also; and if any one would sue you and take your coat, let him have your cloak as well; and if any one forces you to go one mile, go with him two miles. Give to him who begs from you, and do not refuse him who would borrow from you."[7] He later says, "Love your enemies and pray for those who persecute you, so that you may be sons of your Father who is in heaven."[8] So Jesus says ultimately that the Father's love necessitates forgiveness that is unconditional and unlimited, that extends to the greatest enemy that we have.

This "law of love" is a departure from the Old Testament, but notice that the Old Testament is moving toward it. For example, the prophets are getting the idea of mercy being greater than sacrifice,[9] but it is Jesus Who brings the idea of "mercy" to its unconditional end—to its shocking fulfillment, taking away the right of retribution and saying that the Christian should not do that. It was shocking. But it is also a truth that saves the world. It is how we got a court system that could actually implement not only the Silver Rule,[10] but also the Golden Rule.

---

[7] Matt. 5:38–42.
[8] Matt. 5:44–45
[9] Hos. 6:6.
[10] "Do nothing to others that you wouldn't have done to you."

[Doug:] How does that relate to the difference between what we as individuals are called to be versus what "Caesar" as a civil judge might be, because you could say, if that is the case, we can't convict anybody of a crime. We have to forgive them.

This was the challenge faced especially by St. Augustine in *The City of God*. During Augustine's time, Christianity was very popular throughout the whole Roman Empire and was in the process of taking it over because the Empire was slowly crumbling. In that book, Augustine addressed having to reconcile the individual's responsibility with the responsibility of the State and, of course, he struggled mightily trying to balance these two poles. For the individual, he maintained the standard of unrestricted forgiveness. But, Augustine said, the State is in a different position because it also has in its legitimate purview public welfare and safety. It is ethical, for example, to incarcerate a dangerous man who is likely to be a repeat offender. Likewise, as Augustine says, to defend against an aggressive enemy who would destroy your community is part of the State's responsibility. A brilliant theory.

Could you discuss how our relationship with God the Father is different than it is in other major world religions, such as Islam, Judaism, and religions with several gods?

Jesus has changed the whole history of religions in many different ways. The first, which we've already talked about, is Jesus' elevation of the love of the Father to the notion of unlimited, unconditional love. That has been, and still is, a radical change. Christianity is different from other religions in its view of God as unconditional Love. The second thing that Jesus did was to elevate mercy, which exalts forgiveness and compassion above justice. You don't see this done in other religions, where either justice is comparable to love and mercy or is held to be higher than them. Remember, justice has the element of equality in it, so, if one person harms another, the other can repay in a proportional way. Or, if one does something illegal, he should be punished.

In the third place, Jesus substantially diminished punishment theologically. In the early Old Testament, you have God punishing down to the third and fourth generations.[11] That is, it's not just you who are going to be punished for your sins but your children, your grandchildren, and your great-grandchildren. There is nothing like that in Jesus. Indeed, the whole idea of God punishing someone or sending somebody to Hell is completely undermined by Jesus. Instead, He negates that idea, and what we derive from Jesus' teachings is expressed in the *Catechism of the Catholic Church*, which says that Hell is the state of definitive self-exclusion from God and from the blessed. By "self-exclusion" we mean that some people actually *choose* Hell, and that the punishment that we feel for our sins is self-induced. For example, if you go out and get drunk until two o'clock in the morning, and get up the next morning with a hangover, we rarely would say, "God did that to punish me!"

Rather, Jesus teaches us that, at first, it always looks as if the darkness will bring us happiness. That is the whole idea of the devil's seduction or temptation: "I'm going to make you happy because I've got the secret. I know this violates God's covenant, but trust me on this. You are going to be happy." And then, of course, the rug is pulled out from under us. Then we feel the pain of Macbeth for pride, or the pain of Hamlet for anger, or any of the endless permutations of the pain of our sinfulness that comes. So, the idea of God as a punishing God is almost eradicated by Jesus, particularly in His words in the Sermon on the Mount, where He

[11] Exod. 20:5.

says that God causes His rain to fall on the just and unjust as well as His sun to shine on the evil and the good.

Our natural response to this is to say, "Well, wait a minute here. I lived a good life, so I should get blessings. That guy lived a bad life, he should be punished." But Jesus teaches us that God is doing everything He can to bring everybody He can into the Kingdom of God. For example, consider Jesus' Parable of the Worker in the Vineyard. There are workers who come in at the ninth hour and get the same pay as everybody else. To the workers who labored all day that seems to violate justice, but the idea for Jesus is that God's foremost desire is to bring us into His salvation because He is an unconditionally loving Father.

So, the idea of God's punishment is diminished by Jesus. He does bring up the notion of punishment when He describes the "weep[ing] and gnash[ing]" of teeth of the "workers of iniquity."[12] But, of course, He brings it up because we punish ourselves. We can actually choose Hell for ourselves, because we're deluded into thinking that Hell is going to make us happy, that domination of others will make us happy, that power will make us happy. Then, we become addicted to domination, to power, to egocentricity, to narcissism, to self-worship, and so on. Jesus says to those people that it will not be what they expect. *If you keep doing these things, you are going to end up weeping and gnashing your teeth.* Even though it looks to you like these things will make you happy, at the end of the day, even in a community where you can dominate people and make their lives a living Hell, even where you can make people pay the price for whatever they do, eventually you will get to go to a place where everybody makes everybody else's life (including your own) a living Hell. In that place, Jesus says, the outcome is

---

[12] Luke 13:27–28.

loneliness, emptiness, alienation, and pain. You are not going to like it. The devil says one thing, but Jesus tells us the truth, yet some of us believe the devil and choose pain. So, Jesus does warn us about the possibility of punishment, but the notion of God having a primary desire for retribution is significantly diminished.

[Doug:] Well, Father, we say that God has unconditional love. But yet even in the case of the Prodigal Son, he needed to come back and take advantage of that love. Isn't that a condition?

A very good question because, in a way, it is a condition. But it is a condition that God made or created within us, namely, the "condition" of free will. Without that "condition," everything we're talking about today would be moot. If you have no freedom, then your love cannot initiate from within you. You have to have the freedom not to love in order to have the freedom to love. And without the freedom to love, your love is not your own; it doesn't initiate from within you. An easier way of looking at it is that the inability to do something unloving means that your love, or lack of it, is programmed into you—you did not choose it.

Why did God make us this way? He wants our love to be our own. He made us in His very image and likeness, creating us to be like Him. Being made in His image and likeness gives us this awesome power of freedom to choose good or evil. That is what makes all the difference. Without freedom of the will, we couldn't be loving, good, or moral. We couldn't be truth pursuing. We would just be mere robots. If you are doing the loving behaviors because you are programmed to do so by God, it is meaningless. But that one "condition" of free will gives us the awesome power of freely choosing love, of being loving, of doing good, and of pursuing the Truth, which is what—or Who—He is.

It seems today that as Christians, we sometimes run the risk of snuggling into a casual, benign relationship with Jesus and God the Father. How is it that Mary and Joseph, as first-century Jews, understood the meaning of a proper relationship with God? Would this [understanding] have changed when Christ came?

It is a good question, but it is hard for me to get in the hearts and minds of Mary and Joseph, so I have to do it by implication.

Mary is a good Old Testament, Old Covenant woman who has an extraordinary—I'm going to call it mystical—relationship with God. She is an extraordinarily humble, extraordinarily holy woman who has a mystical relationship with God and already recognizes mystically the unconditional love of God in her heart. Mary did not have the same mystical relationship as St. Thérèse of Lisieux or St. Teresa of Ávila or Julian of Norwich, or any later saint in the Catholic Church. Hers was way beyond theirs. Bearing that in mind, I do think that Mary recognized the unconditional love of God. There is also the very significant fact that she herself was conceived without Original Sin, which also must have helped her appropriate that understanding of God.

Do I think that Joseph knew in the same way Mary knew? No, I don't think he did, but I do think that Joseph knew to trust Mary. He knew that this woman was special. He not only trusted Mary's having conceived Jesus virginally by God's power; I think he trusted what she told him about God. So, I do think that in a sense, you can say, yes, Mary and Joseph have that sense or awareness of God's unconditional love in a way that is beyond the Old Covenant view of God's love.

As for the other part of the question about "snuggling up to God" and not having a realistic notion about what is going on in the world, there is always a danger that if you talk about the unconditional love of God, people will get the impression that it really doesn't matter what they do. Of course, Jesus never said anything like that. He had two points that He was making side by side. First, God is unconditional Love. God is going to forgive you the minute you come back to Him, even if you come back to Him imperfectly out of fear. He will forgive you and will try to bring you to salvation. There is nothing in God that stands in the way of your salvation. However, simultaneous with that, Jesus said that you are free, and as a free person, you must guard yourself and know that, along with your freedom, there is evil.

Jesus talked about the devil being present and had a prolific ministry of exorcism, in which He was confronted by demons. Jesus said that He was in a battle with Satan. "I saw Satan fall like lightning from heaven."[13] At the end of His life, He defeated Satan definitively in His unconditionally loving self-sacrifice on the Cross. Nevertheless, the devil is active and wants to deceive you and to tempt you into thinking that you don't need to worry about sinning and following God's law and that you can violate God's law without any effect on you or your salvation. In essence, the devil says, "You don't have to worry about God's law or loving your neighbor. I'm telling you right now, you are going to be much happier being an egocentric, narcissistic, domineering, self-worshiping person. And since God is so loving, you will still be saved in the end. Trust me on this."

In response, Jesus tells us to mark His words when He tells us that this is real-world evil and real-world darkness. We're not just fighting flesh and blood. There is a real-world cosmic struggle between good and evil. There is also still evil within ourselves from Original Sin that opens us to succumb to all of the devil's temptations, so we

[13] Luke 10:18.

need to learn God's law, do our best to follow it, ask for God's grace to help us, and when we fail, avail ourselves of God's forgiving love to redeem us, save us, and to bring us into the heavenly kingdom.

Father, speaking of unconditional love: recently one of our major politicos described certain people that they didn't particularly like as "deplorable," and went on further to say "irredeemable." Is there anybody irredeemable in the mind of Christ and in the Church?

In the mindset of God, according to Jesus Christ, no one is irredeemable. The word *redeemable* means "capable of being saved." This means capable of being reconfigured so that your heart will willingly and lovingly accept God and the blessed in Heaven. In that sense, nobody is irredeemable. Even Hitler, who may look like he was irredeemable, was not irredeemable until he refused salvation in the end. If he repented and had a sincere change of heart, then he would have been redeemable. God could use that even for Hitler. You or I might not think Hitler repented, but only God knows, Hitler might have repented, and if so, God would have responded. So, the answer is no, nobody is irredeemable in the eyes of God.

[Doug:] Do you think that this, in some way, ties into the Prodigal Son story, in the sense that the Pharisees, who feel like they are doing their best to live out their lives, don't want the other person to get off the hook so easily? That is, they want to limit God's mercy because they believe they have been doing the right thing, and then this guy [the prodigal] just slides in. The parable indicates that, if we truly love God, we should be rejoicing that our brother is back and not be jealous that he may be "getting away with something."

Yes, and in fact, this is part of Jesus' challenge to the Pharisees. He pointed out their inauthenticity in laying heavy burdens on men's shoulders and not lifting a finger to help them.[14] Further, the Pharisees were basically telling people to give up on salvation because their sins made them irredeemable. Jesus gets angriest when He hears the religious authorities saying this because it misrepresents God's view and discourages people from seeking the mercy that God wants to extend to them. Jesus is also concerned that the Pharisees by their bad faith are harming themselves in the process. He uses the parable about the late workers to show God's generosity in wanting to save those who freely come to Him. So, He is saying to the Pharisees, "Who are you to tell me what to do with my money? Are you jealous that I am generous? Do you want to get what they get plus more? Your viewpoint is a complete misunderstanding of my heart. I'm going to save everybody that I can save who willingly comes to me, accepts me, and wants to follow me. That is my objective."

There are a lot of people out there who preach the terrifying, retributive God who punishes down to the fourth generation because in some sense, they want to count their righteousness as being greater than the righteousness of latecomers to the faith. Jesus teaches that we should be rejoicing if somebody comes late to the faith, even as much as one second before death. We should rejoice and not be depressed because somebody got more than we did.

[Doug:] Or got the same without having to pay the dues. As if heavenly reward is a zero-sum game – because somebody gets something good, he must be taking something away from me.

---

[14] See Matt. 23:4.

I Believe in Jesus Christ, Our Lord

Crucified under Pontius Pilate

Last week you touched on the Creed. We were talking about the Eucharist. Why do you suppose Pontius Pilate's name was included in the Creed? It bothers me how many times a day his name is repeated throughout the world. Why call so much attention to him when it was all of us that caused Christ to suffer?

[Doug:] I guess somebody is asking why we are putting all of the blame on Pontius Pilate?

We're not putting all the blame on Pilate. But at the Council of Nicaea in particular, in order to establish that Jesus not only was true God but also true man, it was very important to locate Jesus' Incarnation, death, and Resurrection at a particular place and time. The most evident historical indicator of His place and time is the reign of Pontius Pilate, who was the governor in Israel of the Judean Roman colony between A.D. 26 and 36. This is the temporal indicator the Church used to show Jesus' historicity, which was important for establishing the time of His Crucifixion and Resurrection.

You're right, there were a lot of other people who were involved in Jesus' trial and Crucifixion—not just Pilate, but his notoriety made him the best one to indicate Jesus' historicity.

[Doug:] I never thought of it that way. It all occurred at a point in time in history, and the Creed recalls this so that people know that this was a real event.

That is right. It is a definitive historical indicator. And there are a variety of extrabiblical sources like Josephus and the Roman historian, Tacitus, who both testify to the historicity of Jesus, and who, with the Gospels, converge on this one name, Pontius Pilate.

Josephus's Reliability

As an aside, do you think Josephus was a Roman collaborator?

I think he certainly was a Roman cooperator because he was working for the emperor. Nevertheless, he had very strong feelings for Judaism and for Jerusalem. However, he did want to make his three major works appealing to the Roman populace for which he was writing and was being rewarded handsomely. I do think he makes it appealing, and he explains a lot of things; but he is in many ways Jewish, but within the Roman culture. So he is certainly not endorsing zealotry, but he presents a lot of the Jewish movements, even those that were no friends of Rome, and on these he is somewhat historically reliable. Josephus is an interesting figure and had a wide readership in Rome and among the Jewish people, so you can say he is sort of lodged in between. He wasn't a collaborator or a denier of the authenticity of Judaism. But he had been secularized: a fact that some people use to question his writing. However, I think he is reliable. He does talk about Jesus, not only in terms of Hs Crucifixion, but also that He was known to be a miracle-worker and of considerable influence. *That*, coming from a Jewish person writing for Romans, means something, even if he was secularized. It means quite a bit.

The Crucifixion: Jesus' Suffering

Did Jesus' divine power have anything to do with the amount of torture and pain He was able to endure, or could a normal person endure that much abuse as well? Also, do you think that Mother Mary knew beforehand that her son would suffer crucifixion?

[Doug:] A person might think, "If I were the Son of God, I could endure it." As a person who doesn't have that power or certainty, crucifixion seems very scary to me. What do you say?

First of all, we have to remember that Jesus Christ is not only true God, He is also true man. When we acknowledge His humanity, we're saying that He really possessed all of the dimensions of a human being, including all of the ability to suffer real pain and anguish in the flesh. This would include the ability to suffer His rejection by the religious authorities and even the denial and flight of His own friends and disciples. In all these things, there was no diminishing of the suffering He experienced. Obviously, Jesus knew the support of the Father, He knew the will of the Father, and was able to offer the prayer in the Garden of Gethsemane, where He said, "My Father, if it be possible, let this cup pass from me; nevertheless, not as I will, but as thou wilt."[15] So, He knew the graces that He had as the divine Son, which gave Him the assurance that the Father was there. But did any of this minimize His suffering? No! Did it give Him extrahuman willpower to endure the suffering? No! He was really a true man with a real human will along with its limitations and abilities, including the capacity to experience pain and torture.

[15] Matt. 26:39.

As for your second question, could a normal human being endure that, the answer is, well ... yes. Consider the Japanese martyrs of Nagasaki. Their tortures were immense. Look at the English martyrs, many of whom were drawn and quartered. Look at the North American martyrs, some of whom were skinned alive. Not to mention the Roman martyrs, torn apart by animals in the Colosseum or enduring crucifixions. Some of them, by the way, were not tied to the cross. Some of them in imitation of Jesus were nailed to their crosses, just for good measure and a little extra torture. So many of the martyrs went through unimaginable tortures. In faith, by the power of the Holy Spirit, they did endure lots of suffering.

But let's consider Jesus' Crucifixion. It was a very unique crucifixion, really the height of torture. Nobody else was crowned with thorns. We know from the Shroud of Turin that it left a large number of wounds in His head, the nape of His neck, and along His face. Then consider the number of whippings that He got. Roman whips had bone chips and metal embedded at the end of the three strands on the whip so that, when they made contact with the skin, they literally ate into the flesh. Then consider the nails. There are many nerve endings that connect where the wrist meets the hand. Imagine getting a huge nail driven right through all those nerves! That alone must have been a torment of unbelievable proportions. Of course, between the torture by scourging and the Crucifixion, He had to carry His Cross. Without Simon of Cyrene, He would never have made it to Golgotha. But with Simon's help, He did get there. When you're nailed to a cross instead of being tied to it, you're essentially going to die a very painful suffocation. Everything inside your body wants you to pull up so you won't suffocate, but when you do pull up, it would have to be by the nails, further aggravating all those nerve endings in the wrist and in your feet: the torture is overwhelming. But you can't help yourself, because you want to breathe. So His executioners had Him caught—not just between a rock and a hard place—but between either pushing up by the nails or suffocating, the latter of which you can't do practically without finally sagging down in utter exhaustion and torment. This is what happened to Him; He endured the Cross alone for three hours.

[Doug:] Where does that description fit into with the idea that we know from Scripture about His hands and the legs not being broken.[16] The Romans would break the legs so that the crucified person couldn't hold themselves upright.

That is right, because eventually you'd get so tired by trying to pull yourself up with your arms. They actually put a little wooden stripe off the vertical of the cross so that you could put your feet on it and sort of push yourself up. That would enable you to last for twenty hours or more, just trying to lift yourself to be able to breathe. But then they got tired of the torture—or, in the case of Jesus' Crucifixion, the next day was Passover—and so, in order to hasten his death, they would break his knees so that he couldn't then lift himself with his legs. He'd have to do it by his arms. Not to mention the added pain of capped knees. So he died very quickly on the cross after his knees were broken. This was not necessary for Jesus because literally He had suffered so much from the scourging, the nails in His wrists, and in the joint between the ankles and the heel that He died early on, after three hours.

[Doug:] Regarding your mention of twenty hours, someone did ask why Our Lord died so quickly. I understand that the Roman soldiers probably

---

[16] John 19:36.

got tired of hanging out at the crucifixion site and wanted to finish them off quickly, which is why they broke their legs. Why did Our Lord last only three hours—was it because of the torture?

Yes, it was because of the torture. The incredible number of lashes administered during the scourging would have created tremendous blood loss and weakening, and the nailing in His hands and feet guaranteed that He would not last long, because every time He pulled Himself up, He was literally being shocked by all these nerve endings. It is similar to a terrible back pain, where you've got pain shooting through you, except instead of being able to lie down or get some support to at least alleviate the pain, everything you do exacerbates the pain. You get shocks all over again in the ankle and wrist joints to the point where it is unbearable. Jesus had to say, "It is finished," and it was because His body just couldn't do it anymore. Then, He sagged on the Cross and, unable to take one more torment of pulling Himself up, He suffocated, expired, and gave up His spirit.

Can you explain why Matthew and Mark write that the thieves next to Jesus mocked Him, even though Luke says one of the thieves stuck up for Him. Also, the Gospel of John says Jesus carried His Cross, while the others say that Simon of Cyrene carried it. Does this kind of discrepancy lend itself to asking why there are conflicting versions; and does that lead to the idea that maybe some of this stuff was made up, so to speak?

Each Gospel has its own sources. Matthew and Luke both depend on Mark, and they share Q[17] as a source, as well. John is a completely

---

[17] Q, for *Quelle* (German "source"), is an unattested document, hypothesized by biblical scholars to account for the many passages shared by Matthew and Luke, but not found in Mark.

independent source. But concerning the Passion narratives, there are a lot of sources interacting throughout. So, first of all, you have Mark's account, which probably comes from Peter, because tradition associates Mark and Peter with one another.[18] Mark may even have been a secretary for Peter, so he is probably reporting Peter's account. For example, Jesus' final words are given in Mark in Northern Galilean Aramaic. That of course would be Jesus' and Peter's native dialect. Matthew on the other hand renders it into the Hebrew so that you will recognize the reference to Psalm 22. But Jesus actually said the Psalm as He would have learned it from His mother as a child, and Peter remembers it that way and tells Mark.

Concerning the thieves, in the Markan version, "those crucified with Him" mock Him. This is what is remembered by Peter, who was not present for the Crucifixion. Luke has, in addition to Mark and Q, special Lukan sources.[19] We should not be surprised if Luke had some other source that indicated there was something else going on, because this kind of thing frequently happens. John has all kinds of incidents in his accounts that are not mentioned in either Matthew or Luke. For example, the spear being thrust into Jesus' side and the outflow of blood and water. You might wonder how he knows that water flowed out from Jesus' side? When Dr. Frederick Zugibe examined the Shroud of Turin, he had at his disposal an actual Roman spear that was used by the Roman legions at that time. Based on the dimensions of the spear as compared to the blood on the Shroud, Dr. Zugibe determined the exact angle through which the spear traveled and into the specific ribs (between

---

[18] See, e.g., 1 Pet. 5:13.

[19] This material that is unique to Luke (e.g., the Parable of the Prodigal Son, Luke 15:11–32) is attributed to a source called *L* by biblical scholars.

the fifth and sixth ribs) and found that it would have hit the pleural sac just after it nicked the heart. Thus, there would have been a flow of blood from the heart and a clear liquid from the pleural sac. Remember, Peter wasn't there; John was. So this explains why the Synoptics do not report this.

However, given the fact that there are roughly three dozen major components of the Crucifixion narratives, when we start from the treachery of Judas before the Last Supper, all the way through to the burial of Jesus and the Resurrection, what is really shocking is that, though they came from different sources—and clearly John likely comes from the Beloved Disciple, Mark probably comes from Peter, and Luke has special sources—what flabbergasts me is, given all of that complexity, how stunningly similar they are—in excruciating detail.

In sum, I think these conflicts are mostly explicable because, again, the Gospel writers have different sources. Those different sources may not remember everything, but they remember an amazing amount of detail.

So, in addition to different points of view, each one had access to different information. We know, though, that one disciple who remains loyal to the end is the one who writes the Fourth Gospel, the Beloved Disciple, who was present there at the foot of the Cross, where Jesus presents His mother to him.

So it's pretty clear that the differences among the accounts— which are minor—can be reconciled. It involves memory, and depends on which witness was there and what they recall.

[Doug:] Almost like reading different newspaper accounts of the same event.

Exactly. If you get in a trial, it's the same—different witnesses remember different things.

[Doug:] You pointed out that John was there at the foot of the Cross. Our understanding is that Peter wasn't present at the Crucifixion, so where would that account come from?

Peter fled. We can only assume that he received the report from one or more of two sources who were there—the Beloved Disciple or one or more of the women who were there. I think Peter is a firsthand witness to just about everything except, of course, when he and most of the disciples decided to flee out of fear.

[Doug:] Sometimes it gets portrayed this way: John would be considered almost like a boy, and the women weren't at the same risk of arrest or trial as the apostles might have been. Is that a correct understanding?

Yes, I think Peter was front and center as a recognized disciple. It may very well have been the same with the other disciples because of their Galilean accents. But it's hard to know for sure with John. Either he decided to take the risk to be there or in some sense decided that the risk was less for him than it was for the other disciples, because Peter was identified immediately when he was in the courtyard outside the Jewish tribunal. It is difficult to say why that happened, but I think they all knew that they could be next.

The rest of the disciples fled. Some scholars think they fled right away to Galilee and that Jesus appeared to them there in the closed room. Luke, however, seems to put the closed room account in Jerusalem. It is difficult to say exactly where they fled to, but ultimately they did go to Galilee, and Jesus certainly did appear to them there and later again in Jerusalem. And it would seem that the appearance to the five hundred may have been in Galilee rather than in Jerusalem, and that the appearance to some of the other apostles might have been in Jerusalem. Of course, the final appearance to the apostles would have been in Jerusalem. It is difficult to say, though, because that is not presented sequentially in the Scriptures. Many scholars have tried to assemble it chronologically, but unless you have exact and historical testimony, it is anybody's guess.

[Doug:] Is it also because the people of that time considered those kinds of things unimportant?

Absolutely. For us, historical sequence is exceedingly important. We want to get exactly what happened and precisely when it happened. For them, the sequence is not as important as the fact that it happened and what else happened within that event. By the time the narratives were being written, there were perhaps hundreds of stories already being formulated about Jesus. There were lots of these stories circulating, and it didn't take long for them to be included in collections. For example, Mark is the first to do a narrative collection. Q is generally regarded as a collection of Jesus' sayings, so you don't really get narrative out of Q. We've already mentioned that Luke has special sources that we don't know. Matthew, too, had special sources that we don't know about.[20] And the Gospel of John, the Beloved Disciple, tells a quite different narrative. He writes his Gospel almost anew from his own experience—not dependent on Mark or Matthew or Luke.

The last part that is really relevant to your question is: Does sequence matter? The answer is a qualified yes: it matters to some extent. For example, the sequence of the Passion would matter because it is one continuous narrative. But other sequences, for

---

[20] Matthew's special sources—those that account for material in Matthew but not in Mark or Luke—are collectively called M. As with Q and L, these sources are hypothetical. No copies of Q, M, or L are extant.

example, Jesus' travels from Galilee up to Jerusalem, are less significant. That is the way history was done. What matters is that the
account actually happened. The actual sequencing is generally at
the liberty of the writer, and according to the preference of what
we call the final redactor. Not sequencing the details would be fine,
as long as a general sequencing is correct. In addition, the writers
take theological liberties: for example, Passion predictions. Did
Jesus make Passion predictions? Absolutely. Did He use Scripture in
making Passion predictions? Absolutely. Are we absolutely certain
that Jesus made the predictions exactly as Mark said He made the
predictions? Not so certain. Mark could have taken the theological
or thematic liberty of inserting a prediction right after the Transfiguration. But even so, I believe that is historical. I believe Jesus,
immediately after the Transfiguration, took the first opportunity to
tell His disciples that, though what the three disciples saw looked
glorious, still the Son of Man must suffer and be persecuted by
the chief priests and the scribes, be put to death, and then rise
again on the third day. Jesus gave them the truth. Is this typical of
Jesus? Yes, it is. So I view that very much as historical.

[Doug:] Is the Transfiguration a preview of what the Resurrection would be?

Absolutely, for two reasons. First of all, the Transfiguration is literally the handing over of the Old Covenant to Jesus. Moses and
Elijah, the great lawgiver and the great prophet, were at the Transfiguration handing over everything to Jesus. At that point, they
are a sort of triumvirate. They're discussing it while in their glory,
and Jesus is taking the baton. The covenant is being handed over
to Him, and that is really important.

Second, it is the prefiguring of the Resurrection. Jesus is already
aware at the time of His Transfiguration that things are going to

go badly. He knows that He is going to be persecuted. And so, the apostles have to be given an assurance of His impeding Resurrection—assurance as well of His glorification and divine Sonship which point to their own resurrection and glory. It is only after the Transfiguration that Jesus speaks clearly to them about His Passion, that the whole story is going to be His self-sacrificial act, which is going to save the world.

Christ's Descent into "Hell"

Did Christ descend into Hell as the Creed says? What did He do there?

[Doug:] I think you hear it translated also "to the dead." But a lot of people ask, what was Jesus doing in Hell? Why did He go there?

This is an unfortunate translation issue involving the Hebrew word *sheol*, which refers to the realm of the dead, and the Greek word *hades*. Maybe you're familiar with the term *hades* from Greek mythology. Hades was the god of the underworld, but the word was also a generic term for the underworld, or the realm of the dead. So, in the New Testament, Greek *hades* was understandably used to represent the concept of the Hebrew *sheol*.

Now, what did the Israelite people believe about the realm of the dead? They didn't have a very clear idea of it at all. They believed that *sheol* was the place where people went after they had died. There, they had a shadowy existence. It is important to note that this is not the same notion of Hell that we described elsewhere, where people have made a definitive self-exclusion from communion with God.

Between the time of the Crucifixion and the Resurrection, Jesus already had victory over the devil and over sin. It was at that time that He went to liberate all of the people from the domain of *sheol.* Jesus' descent was for the purpose of liberating every single person who could be justified and made righteous, because they followed the Lord by the dictates of their conscience—as the Second Vatican Council tells us. When the Lord went down into the domain of the dead right after His Crucifixion, He liberated every one of the righteous from that domain where they were awaiting the time of the fulfillment of salvation and brought them into His heavenly kingdom.

By the way, the last of Jesus' Nine Words ("It is finished"—John 19:30) recall the very last line of Psalm 22: "He has wrought it" (v. 31b). But verses 29–31 of that psalm imply the liberation of those "who go down to the dust." "The dust" is the domain of *sheol,* and so that psalm tells us something about His descent into *sheol* to liberate the just, whom He then brought into heaven.

I Believe in Life Everlasting

Predestination and Free Will

In our Catholic Church, I believe it is said that we have the ability to make our own choices. Yet how do we make our own life choices with God already knowing the destiny of our soul?

[Doug:] So, the whole idea of predestination, control, election vs. free will.

This gets into what is probably the most complex theological question that there is. It is called "God's knowledge of future contingents." The Church is clear on this: God does know what our destiny is. You ask, "How can that be? I'm in the present moment. It is my free choice in the present moment. How is God aware of every decision that I haven't made yet if I am truly free?"

The Church answers that God's notion of time is different from our notion of time. God's awareness of the full context of the horizon of time is very different from our viewpoint of the unfolding of our choices in the present moment. God doesn't see the unfolding of our present choices as something that is happening in the future. He sees the unfolding of our choices through a nontemporal "lens," as it were, that actually enables Him to collapse into a single moment the variety of choices that you are making over the course of what we perceive to be the passage of time, which God is not limited by. So, we can continuously and freely choose things in the present, as we see ourselves going into the future. God, however, doesn't see our future as His future , but as His *present*, because as St. Augustine said, "He is in an eternal now"—a transtemporal (beyond time) existence. Thus, He sees the whole of time, the eternal now as a single reality (rather than a progressing or continuing one). Though we perceive ourselves in an ongoing and unfolding progression, God sees us in a transtemporal singularity in which His knowledge does not determine what we perceive to be our future. We cannot deny this possibility of a transtemporal reality like God without making Him a temporalized reality. This is the vexing problem of future contingents. We are so locked into our temporalized view of reality that we cannot understand the perspective of a transtemporal reality without demoting the transtemporal reality to our temporalized one. So, we have to decide. Do we want to temporalize the transtemporal in order for us to understand it—or do we want, in all humility, to let God be God and accept that we are not God and cannot understand His transtemporal perspective? The choice is ours.

Now, the Protestant reformer John Calvin got really stuck on this. He could not fathom this view of a future that was not unfolding for God as it is unfolding for us in a temporal succession. Because he couldn't conceive of this, he really thought that God's awareness of the future would have to condition the choices that we make in our present. However, if God's transtemporal awareness of reality does not undermine our sense of time in making our choices, then His transtemporal knowledge of our choices does not determine our temporalized future. As I said above, it is impossible for us to understand how this can work without being in God's transtemporal condition. Every time we try to understand it, we temporalize God's perspective which prevents us from understanding it as it is. All we can do is acknowledge the rational possibility of a transtemporal view of reality which need not determine our temporalized experience of it. Calvin did not acknowledge that possibility and, consequently, he really believed that we were completely predestined and that free choice was really an illusion because it was canceled out by God's knowledge of future contingents.

[Doug:] So you can't say that the devil made me do it or God made me do it. Because it is basically your decision.

Right. Neither can you appeal to fatalism. Calvin's doctrine gets into fatalism without question. It teaches that the whole of life is a *fait accompli.*

[Doug:] It is basically going through the motions.

Purgatory

Could you provide a clear biblical reference for the existence of Purgatory as it is taught in our Faith? Where is it referenced in Scripture?

This is a legitimate question because we didn't get a strong declaration of the notion of Purgatory until the Middle Ages. The doctrine of Purgatory was based on the biblical idea of atonement after death, and the fully developed doctrine is viewed as *purification* after death, where after death you are assured of your salvation, but you are also in need of some purification before entering Heaven. Human freedom plays an important part in the definition of that doctrine.

The first question, then, is what evidence is there in the Old Testament? If you turn to 2 Maccabees 12:41–46,[21] which was

---

[21] The Catholic Church, along with the Eastern Orthodox and some Anglicans, has always accepted the books of the Maccabees as part of her canon of Scripture, i.e., as part of the Bible.

written roughly 100 B.C.—and so very close to the time of Jesus—you find that Judas Maccabeus's surviving forces, who had just defeated Gorgias in battle, made atonement—an offering—for those who had fallen in battle. Many of those who had died were discovered to be wearing idolatrous tokens, which was a great sin. So they prayed that the sin might be forgiven, and Judas took up a huge collection, and sent it to the Temple in Jerusalem as a sin offering on behalf of the fallen. That pretty much tells you where intertestamental Judaism was going during the time of Jesus. Jesus would have been familiar with this custom.

During Jesus' time, there were three major "parties": Pharisees, Sadducees, and Essenes. The Sadducees believed only in the Torah, the five books of Moses. They believed that there is no life after death, and therefore no resurrection since it is not mentioned in the Torah. However, the Sadducees were a minority party. They were greatly outnumbered by the Pharisees, who assuredly believed in the resurrection from the dead because of the Old Testament prophetic and wisdom books that witnessed to it. As for the Essenes, they too were a minority, almost like a cult during Jesus' time. They also believed in the resurrection from the dead based on the teaching of one they called "the Teacher of Righteousness."

So, when Jesus came on the scene, He inherited a widespread belief not only in the resurrection from the dead, but also in the possibility of atonement and offerings after death for a person who might have died in sin. Furthermore, in Matthew 12:32, Jesus speaks of the sin against the Holy Spirit. Jesus says, "Whoever says a word against the Son of man will be forgiven; but whoever speaks against the Holy Spirit will not be forgiven, either in this age or in *the age to come*." Well, what is the age to come? And what are we to make of the idea of being forgiven in the age to come? The idea of age— in Greek *eon* or *aeon*—essentially means a span of time. "This age" would refer to our lifetime. But very explicitly Jesus differentiates our lifetime from "the age to come," that is to say, during the time after this lifetime, an *aeon* that generally refers to a future life after death. So, Jesus is explicitly saying that there is the possibility of forgiveness after our lifetime. That is very clearly set out in Scripture. I don't see how you could interpret it in any other way.

Another bit of evidence can be found in St. Paul's Second Letter to Timothy. In this particular case, 2 Timothy 1, Paul writes to Timothy that he is praying for Onesiphorus, who had been of great help to Paul by coming to visit him in prison. Paul writes, "May the Lord grant mercy to the household of Onesiphorus, … [and] may the Lord grant him to find mercy from the Lord on that Day" (vv. 16-18). Essentially, Paul is offering prayers for Onesiphorus's salvation after he has died. Paul asks for mercy for his household, but for Onesiphorus himself he asks for mercy "on that Day," that is, the Day of Judgment. Paul seems to be following the teaching of Jesus in Matthew 12:32.

Let me go one step deeper. If you look archaeologically at what was going on in the early Church, you see numerous etchings on tombs, where people are promising prayers for their dead loved ones. These are Christians who are promising prayers for their dead. This is within ten years after Jesus' Resurrection. There is very clear evidence that the Christian Church in fact encouraged people to pray for their deceased loved ones, including on special days, for example, the third day after a person's death—then the seventh day, the ninth day, the thirtieth day, and the fortieth day after their death. Pray for what? Pray that God will extend forgiveness and mercy to them *after* their death.

You may ask how that actually proves the doctrine of Purgatory as the Church defined it. The answer is, it does so very clearly if you believe in atonement after death. If you believe that there is a possibility of forgiveness after death, then you can certainly believe that God can purify you after death. So, when the medieval Church took up this topic, she took it up in the spirit that after a person dies, if they arrive in need of purification, they are assured of their salvation. They are not going to Hell. They are going to Heaven. Nevertheless, they need purification before they can enter the heavenly kingdom. Why so?

It involves the notion of freedom. We are free beings, and God can't simply make us love Him and one another in a completely non-egotistical and authentic way. He will never try to force this on us. We must freely choose it and accept the purification needed to get there. This takes us back to the notion of inordinate attachments. When people die, they can be inordinately attached to various kinds of things which are going to disrupt the purity of their love. It will disrupt the purity of the joy that will take place in the heavenly kingdom. Such attachments prevent us from looking at another human being through the eyes of Jesus. In that state, I am hanging onto something: maybe honors, or pride, or material things, or power, or dominion, or the ego. I'm hanging on to *something*, and I'm going to have to deal with it freely. I'm going to have to make free choices to detach from it.

[Doug:] Concerning Purgatory, it is Catholic dogma, that is, something that Catholics have to believe. Is that right, Father?

It was defined as a doctrine, so yes, Catholics must believe it.

Jesus said to the thief on the cross that they would be together in Paradise that day. I'm assuming He is talking about the good thief. Was there no Purgatory for the thief? Was the thief a saint? How does that work?

There are two types of contrition, or sorrow for sin: perfect contrition, which arises out of love for God and a purity of motive, and imperfect contrition, which arises out of fear, fear of the loss of Heaven, fear of Hell, or fear of punishment, which causes us to turn and throw ourselves on the mercy of God. If we have sinned and made an imperfect contrition and intend to go to Confession, and if we die before we are able to confess, that fear would likely be sufficient to enter Purgatory, but may not be sufficient to purify our love so that we can enter into the perfect love in the Kingdom of Heaven. Even if we do confess out of fear (imperfect contrition), this does not mean our love will be purified. And if it were not, we would again need additional purification in Purgatory.

If that thief on the cross were imperfectly contrite, that is, he said what he said out of fear, there would be some purification necessary. But this thief is an interesting fellow. He defended Jesus, and he admitted that he deserved the punishment that he was getting. He then turns to Jesus and says, "Remember me when you come in your kingly power."[22] That was an act of faith. He threw himself on the mercy of God through Jesus. He saw something in Jesus that was intrinsically good and worthy of defending. In that case, Jesus judged him right there as having a purity of motive and says, "Truly, I say to you, today you will be with me in Paradise."[23] When in death you have a perfect contrition, you don't go to Purgatory. You actually go straight to Heaven because you've already given up all inordinate attachments. We believe that this is what happens to our saints. They die with perfect contrition, and once they are declared canonized, meaning that there is evidence from

[22] Luke 23:42.
[23] Luke 23:43.

a holy life and miracles that they are in Heaven, we ask for their prayers now because we believe they are in Heaven, *now*.

[Doug:] This next question is going to dovetail right into what you've just said: "Father, did the apostles Paul and Peter have to go to Purgatory before they became saints?"

Good question! Saints are those whose love is perfected to that of Christ. That is to say, they are in their inner being a righteous holy person. The Church has always declared that martyrdom done with purity of faith is a true testimony to the martyr's righteousness, that is to say, their purity of love. Martyrdom is the testimony to the authenticity of the martyr's love for the Lord, that the martyr didn't deny Him, but stuck with Him even at the very cost of his or her life. Sts. Peter and Paul were both Church founders who lived publically, heroically virtuous lives, died a martyr's death, and had many intercessory miracles attributed to them upon their deaths. Therefore, we can be quite sure that they went directly to Heaven and did not go to Purgatory.

[Doug:] Okay. So let's go to another question, one that is partial to what you just talked about:
> *Dear Fr. Spitzer, if someone is in mortal sin but willingly dies as a martyr for the Faith, will they automatically go to Heaven? To Hell? Will God allow him or her to make amends in Purgatory?*

If they are in the state of mortal sin and intent on giving their lives for Christ, we have to presume that, at the very least, they are perfectly contrite for that mortal sin. Otherwise, why in the world would they give their lives for Christ? Why not take the easy path to deny Christ and to escape torture and the death penalty? But these people obviously gave their lives; they didn't deny Christ;

they didn't try to escape the death penalty; and they didn't escape death. So, the answer to that question would be yes, like Baptism by water, forgiveness and redemption come from the shedding of one's blood for Christ. Even if they were only imperfectly contrite before, by giving their lives, they are already perfectly contrite and in Heaven. They certainly don't go to Hell.

Near-Death Experiences

In your book God So Loved the World, *you discuss a correlation between the new transphysical form of near-death experiences and Jesus' risen appearances. Could you please elaborate on this?*

[Doug:] You were talking about this with the Shroud of Turin.

I would say a couple of things. First, Jesus has a glorified spiritual (transphysical) body . In contrast, the persons who have near-death experiences are not glorified, but they do have a spiritual (transphysical) form. So, there is actually a difference. Glorification goes beyond becoming spiritual (transphysical). In brief, it means transformation in power and majesty—becoming "God-like" in appearance.[24] When the apostles saw Jesus' glorified body, they bowed down and worshipped Him.[25] N. T. Wright did a study of Second Temple Judaism, which lasted from roughly 500 B.C. until the destruction of the Temple in A.D. 70. During that time, certain doctrines informally developed, one of which taught that when you are raised from the dead in the general resurrection, it will be a resuscitation of your physical body, except that it would

[24] See 1 Cor. 15:42–44.
[25] Matt. 28:17.

now be incorruptible. Though there were Christians who didn't want to deviate at all from Second Temple Judaism, the Church quickly deviated from Second Temple Jewish thinking almost exclusively in this regard, teaching that our resurrected body will be a "spiritual body," a phrase that St. Paul uses specifically.[26] Our bodies are going to be like the body of the Risen Jesus.[27] When the apostles saw the Risen Christ, His was not just a physical body made spiritual. His was a spiritual *and* glorified body. Paul says in this regard that we are going to be like Jesus[28] We're going to have spiritual bodies that are also glorified like that of Jesus.

This partially parallels what we find with near-death experiences. People who are in that spiritual "form" after they have left their body can go right up to and through the roof; they can pass through walls. A person in that state is not subject to the laws of physics, even when they are still in the world. This is clearly a correlation with Jesus' risen state. But there is another critical way that such a person's state doesn't correlate with Jesus', and that is that Jesus is glorified. He is powerful, beautiful, and divine-like in appearance.[29] When He appeared to the apostles, they thought they were seeing God,[30] and they were right. Even John, the beloved disciple and guardian of the Mother of God, bowed down before Jesus in fear.[31]

In Matthew's Gospel, the devil asks Jesus to worship him, but of course, Jesus says no! "Worship the Lord your God and him only shall you serve."[32] The word *worship* is rarely used, yet in the

---

[26] 1 Cor. 15:44.
[27] 1 Cor. 15:49.
[28] 1 Cor. 15:49.
[29] Matt. 28:17.
[30] John 20:28.
[31] Rev. 1:17.
[32] Matt. 4:10.

description of Jesus' appearance to the disciples, they are bowing down and worshiping Him. There is clearly present something very much beyond the transphysical near-death experience: glorification.

[*Doug:*] *Two related questions:*

> *Does the* Catechism *address the near-death experience, or is there a teaching on the theology of the near-death experience? It seems that, with this near-death experience, Jesus is offering us a modern olive branch with our stubborn minds.*

And the other question is:

> *If we're supposed to die once and be judged, how do we have a near-death experience and return? Why aren't we judged at that time?*

With respect to the first question, I couldn't put it any better. I totally agree that God is giving us, as it were, the olive branch, one more testimony against the stubborn materialism of our times. The *Catechism* doesn't have specific teachings on near-death experience. But I try in my book, *The Soul's Upward Yearning*, to give you a good description of it, and to give you the parallels with Christian theology in that other book, *God So Loved the World*. So, if you just go to the chapter on Jesus' Resurrection, you'll find the parallels that I adduce.

I would add that there is another parallel besides the transphysical aspect of our souls: that Jesus talks about a resurrection into unconditional love, and that resurrection of unconditional love is verified in near-death experiences. In a large number of near-death experiences that go to a beautiful otherworldly domain, patients encounter a "loving white light" that is incomprehensively loving and beautiful, which most patients identify as God or Christ.

I would, however, issue a caution. Be wary of *anecdotal* descriptions of near-death experiences. There are a lot of people out there who are using these things in a very manipulative way. If somebody known to you and trustworthy says to you, "I had a near-death experience," and tells you the story, you can believe that story. But even so, exercise caution, particularly if you hear something that sounds really goofy or contrary to Christian doctrine. There could be a manipulative agenda. Stick with the science; stick with the peer-reviewed studies from hospitals that have excellent research, published in reputable journals. If you stick with the good studies, you are not likely to be misled, and these good studies attest to the loving white light who patients identify as God or Christ.

Christ's Real Presence in the Eucharist

I have a Baptist friend who strongly believes that Holy Communion is just symbolic of Christ's love. How can I better show her the True Presence found in the Eucharist? How would you approach explaining this truth?

[Doug:] Obviously, it is not unusual in the Protestant world to see the Eucharist, or the Lord's Supper, as being totally symbolic. That is not just a Protestant thing: there has actually been a struggle from time to time, even in our own Church, making sure people don't start to think that we're only talking about a sign as purely symbolic as opposed to a sign that wholly contains and imparts what it represents.

The main thing to remember is that it is *historical* that Jesus' intention is to be really present in the species of bread and wine. I have written about this extensively in my book *God So Loved the World*, and in chapter 3 of that book, I have an entire section on why the Protestant interpretation of the Eucharist in history is completely wrong. But to give a brief synopsis of it, remember that Jesus was operating within His Semitic milieu: He is a prophet Who reveals Himself to be the Messiah and the exclusive Son of the Father. So, when He was doing the rite of the bread (the rite of His Body) and the rite of the red wine after the Last Supper (the rite of His Blood), He uses a specifically Semitic view of time, which allows a future event to be brought into the present and a past event to be brought into the present.

Since, for Jesus, all time exists in God, God can transcend the structure of time. Thus, when Jesus did the rite of the bread, He was speaking in a prophetic way, specifically the prophetic future. This is more difficult for us to understand because we look at time as an invariant reality underlying physical events. But for Jesus time is collapsible because it exists through the mind of God, Who can reconfigure it according to His will. This means that He can take the time between the present moment (at the Last Supper) and a future event (His Crucifixion) and collapse it so that the substance of the event in the future (Jesus' Body hanging from the Cross) can become present in the bread He is handing to His disciples at the Supper. He does this by His prophetic pronouncement as the Messiah and the Son of God. Note that this was not just His prophetic pronouncement, but also His divine pronouncement: "This is my Body given for you." The very second that He expressed that in the present tense, He literally collapsed the future moment, namely His Crucifixion, into the species of the bread that He was handing to His disciples, transforming that species into His crucified Body. That is the context out of which He is operating.

You might be thinking, "Hey, wait a minute. At the Last Supper Jesus' Crucifixion was in the future, which hadn't happened yet. How could He take His Body on the Cross, which has not occurred, and bring it into the bread He is passing to His disciples at the Last Supper on Thursday?" Recall that all time is in God and that all future events are viewed by God within His "eternal now"—His awareness of the whole of time as a transtemporal singularity. This means that Jesus' prophetic-divine announcement can reach into the future (existing in the Divine mind) and bring His future Body hanging on the Cross into the bread He is giving to His disciples at the Last Supper.

Jesus' notion of time is different from ours because it is completely within the power of God. The same thing is true of the rite of the wine, which became His Blood. He collapsed the time between the future event of His Blood being poured out on the Cross and the present moment at the Supper. He collapsed it so that the Blood pouring from His Body on Good Friday became present in the wine He was handing to His disciples on Thursday. This collapse of time is indicated by Jesus' use of the present passive participle—translated in Greek as *ekchunnomenon* (*is being* poured out). This implies that His Blood is being poured out *now* (at the Last Supper) even though this event (according to our perception of time) is still in the future (on Friday).[33] That is one-half of the story. The other half is that Jesus understood time to also be collapsible between the present and the past because it, too, is governed by divine power. Thus, Jesus (following the ancient Semitic understanding of time and His awareness of His Father's power over time) did not view "remembrance" as a merely intellectual "calling to mind." Rather, He viewed "remembrance" as a reliving of a past sacred event so that that past event could be made real in the present moment. Thus, when a priest relives a sacred event, his words collapse the time between his present moment and the past sacred event, making the past sacred event real in the present moment. This is what Jesus meant by "Do this in memory of me." So, for example, when a priest says Mass this very day, he, *in persona Christi*,[34] is collapsing time. And when he says the words of the Consecration at the altar, he collapses the time

---

[33] Matt. 26:28, Mark 14:24, Luke 22:20.

[34] *In persona Christi*, Latin for "in the person of Christ," indicates the fact that, by his ordination, a priest is ontologically configured to Christ, so that what he, the priest, does, Christ Himself is doing.

between the past event (the Crucifixion and Last Supper) and the present moment (at the Mass). Jesus intended that the priest use the same prophetic words through the power that He gave to His apostles and to their successors in order to collapse the time from the present back into past: the Crucifixion and the Last Supper.

Therefore, in the Mass, Jesus' crucified Body is becoming present in that species of bread, and His Blood pouring from the Cross is becoming present in the species of wine, by means of the words of the Consecration — in the prophetic pronouncement — spoken by the priest.

This is what Jesus meant by the Greek *anamnesis*, which means "remembrance." The Jewish people had no notion of a mere *mental* remembrance, which is a Greek notion. What Jesus intends for the Last Supper is the same idea present in the Hebrew mind of the Old Testament in which the father of a household at the Passover table recites the words of Passover and answers the questions of the youngest son, dressed as if in a hurry to leave. They, too, are collapsing the time between their present event (the celebration of Passover) and the past sacred event (the historical Passover that finally enabled the Israelites to escape from Egypt). But in the case of the Eucharist, it is animated not just with prophetic words but with Jesus' own divine intention to make present His Crucified and Risen Body in the Host that is being elevated by the priest today. Furthermore, Jesus' Risen presence is also conjoined to the Crucified presence that the priest is effecting by collapsing the time between his words and the past moments of Jesus' Crucifixion and Last Supper. *All* of it comes into the bread and the wine of Consecration, the literal Body and Blood of Christ.

I have explained this with extensive footnotes and details from good scholarly articles going back to the time of Gerhard von Rad in his fine book *Old Testament Theology: Volume 2*, from Joachim

Jeremias's *Eucharistic Words of Jesus*, and from the second volume of Catholic exegete John P. Meier's multivolume *A Marginal Jew*. A very concise and clear summary is given in Johannes Betz's article "Eucharist" in *Sacramentum Mundi*. This is real history and real hermeneutics. Anyone who tells you that the Greek view of *anamnesis* as mere "calling to mind" is adequate for understanding Jesus' divine, prophetic, and Semitic intention is simply wrong. Such people are not looking at history; they are not looking at contemporary hermeneutics and exegesis. We have more than enough evidence to conclude that what Jesus intended to convey at the Last Supper was His real Crucified and Risen Body and Blood.

I might add that this view of the real presence of Christ's Body and Blood in the Eucharist is evident in the Eucharistic discourse of John 6:31–59. How can anyone read the words, "The bread which I shall give for the life of the world is my flesh" (John 6:51) and interpret it in any other way than the bread we receive at Communion truly is His flesh. Jesus could have said, "is symbolic of my flesh," but He did not. He could have said, "represents my flesh," but He did not. He could have said, "is similar to my flesh," but He did not. He said, "is (*estin*) my flesh," which was as close to identity or equivalence as He could get. How can any exegete claim otherwise?

I might also point out that this same understanding of real presence is held by virtually every early Church father—for example, St. Ignatius of Antioch (A.D. 110),[35] St. Justin Martyr (A.D. 151),[36] St. Irenaeus (A.D. 189),[37] St. Ambrose of Milan (A.D. 390),[38] and

---

[35] St. Ignatius of Antioch, *Letter to the Romans* 7:3.

[36] St. Justin Martyr, *First Apology* 6.

[37] St. Irenaeus, *Against Heresies* 4:33 and 5:2.

[38] St. Ambrose of Milan, *On the Mysteries* 9:50, 58.

St. Augustine (A.D. 405).[39] Did these and so many other Church Fathers get a false interpretation of what Jesus meant at the Last Supper or in John's Eucharistic discourse? Very unlikely.

Finally, I should add that there are three contemporary scientifically investigated Eucharistic miracles (Buenos Aires, 1996; Tixtla, Mexico 2006; and Sokolka, Poland 2008), which together give striking evidence of living and wounded heart tissue growing out of the substance of a consecrated Host. The substance of the Host and the substance of the heart tissue are interconnected on the level of the thin filaments of the myofibrils (on the level of a few cell lengths), which no human technology—not even at NASA—can possibly replicate. In other words, it cannot be fraudulently produced. I have written about this extensively, with recourse to the examining scientists and lab reports, in *Christ, Science, and Reason* (chapter 4).[40]

One last question surrounding this issue: "Did Jesus truly view Himself as the Son of God?" Absolutely. Jesus called Himself the Son of Man—referring back to Daniel 7:9-14, where the Son of Man is coming on His throne from Heaven—this Son of Man was viewed as existing with God before Creation and would be coming into the world with all of God's angels surrounding Him in order to be the definitive Judge of the world. This is what Jesus calls Himself in front of the crowds and Pharisees. He also said privately to His disciples, "No one knows the Son except the Father, and no one knows the Father except the Son and any one to whom the Son chooses to reveal him."[41] Notice that for Semites, knowing is

---

[39] St. Augustine, *Explanations of the Psalms* 33:1:10.

[40] Robert J. Spitzer, *Christ, Science, and Reason: What We Can Know about Jesus, Mary, and Miracles* (San Francisco: Ignatius Press, 2024), 159-190.

[41] Matt. 11:27.

not merely mental activity; it is also a loving, personal, conjoining unity of being with the Father. This is the Semitic mentality, and so we have to break out of the Greek categories of thinking that we inherited. We must move back into the categories of Jesus in order to understand His intention. When we do, we can see that Jesus meant by the above proclamation, "I know the Father as the Father knows me." This is definitely a statement of His divinity and coexistence with the Father.

Furthermore, Jesus raised the dead (a power belonging to God alone) by His own authority, saying, "*I say to you, arise*" (Luke 7:11–17—the widow of Nain, and Matt. 9:18–26—the raising of Jairus's daughter). In doing these things, He broke with the tradition of all the prophets, who never claimed to heal by their own authority but asked God to send *His* power to work through them. Jesus also claimed to have the authority to fulfill the law, bring the Kingdom of God in His own Person, and to defeat evil by His own authority, all of which were reserved by Israel's religious authorities to *Yahweh* alone.[42] I have explained this matter in detail in *Science, Reason and Faith: Discovering the Bible* (NT#7), In conclusion, don't be misled by second-rate scholarship, second-rate history, and second-rate hermeneutics that don't recognize Jesus' Jewish background or implicitly deny His prolific miraculous power to heal, exorcise, and raise the dead by His own authority.

[Doug:] Even in some parts of the Catholic world people wonder about the necessity of the priesthood. That is obviously why you don't see the priesthood in the other denominations. There is also Jesus' Eucharistic

---

[42] See N. T. Wright, *Jesus and the Victory of God* (Minneapolis: Fortress Press, 1996), 649–651.

Discourse,[43] *where the crowd responds that this is a hard teaching. Well, if the Eucharist is just a sign, why would it be so hard? And we know from early Christian apologists and from historians that the early Church was being accused of cannibalism.*

You're absolutely correct, Doug. The Eucharistic Discourse gives you a very good idea of what the early Church taught. There is no question that the preponderance of evidence in John's Gospel points to Jesus' real Body and Blood in the Eucharistic bread and cup, where Jesus says, "The bread which I shall give for the life of the world is *my flesh*" (John 6:51) and "My flesh is food *indeed*, and my blood is drink *indeed*" (John 6:55). "*My*." You cannot get any more definitive about Jesus' presence in this matter. But, there's more. You can go right through the other three Gospels and see the definitive expression of Jesus' *own* Body and Blood expressed in the present tense of "to be" — *estin* (expressing identity or equivalence) in Matthew, Mark, and Luke.[44] Furthermore, recall from above, the use of the present passive participle — *ekchunnomenon* (*is being* poured out) in Matthew, Mark, and Luke,[45] implying that it is being poured out *in the present moment* at the Last Supper. This indicates the collapse of time explained above. As we saw above, this is certainly the understanding of the early Church Fathers. Thus, it is evident that the Eucharistic bread and cup was viewed by both the apostolic Church and early Church Fathers as the real Body and Blood of Christ.

Father, how would we explain transubstantiation to a materialist, since there is no evidence of molecular change?

---

[43] John 6, where Jesus repeatedly insists that one must eat His Flesh and drink His Blood to have life.

[44] Matt. 26:26–28; Mark 14:22–24; Luke 22:19.

[45] Matt. 26:28; Mark 14:24; Luke 22:20.

In order to understand transubstantiation, you have to become acquainted with Aristotelian metaphysical terms, which were well-known in the time of St. Thomas Aquinas. Today, they are less known. However, they are still quite valid. You would therefore have to be willing to take time with your materialist friend to explain these metaphysical terms. Briefly, the key terms are *substance* and *accidents*. These words are present in contemporary English, but with meanings different from those in Aristotle.

Substance refers to the underlying reality of a thing. *Accidents* are all of the various characteristics that control the way in which something *appears* and how it manifests itself in the material world. So, when we say *transubstantiation*, we're saying the thing's *substance* has been transformed, not its accidents. So, all of the things that give rise to an appearance in the material world — for example, the atomic, subatomic, molecular, and other constructs; what we might call governing characteristics that shape the appearance *around* the substance — those things don't change.

For example, if you were to look at a consecrated Host under the microscope, you would still see molecules that constitute bread; it would be identical to an unconsecrated wafer. If you broke the Host down even further into atomic constituents, you would see different kinds of carbon compounds and bonding characteristic of bread. It would be the same if you could look at it with an electron microscope. To all appearances, that is, to all accidents, it is bread. The Church teaches that there is no change in physical appearance or in any of the laws or characteristics that constitute the physical appearance of bread. At the same time, we do hold that there is something more than physical appearance. There is an underlying fundamental reality that we would call *substance* that gives the essential power for what philosophers call "higher levels of being." For example, Aristotle distinguished four major levels of substance/being—merely material substances; living substances; self-moving substances (with sensate consciousness); and immaterial/spiritual substance (which is the only kind that can be self-conscious and rational). We can go even further and talk about higher levels of spiritual substance, such as would be found in angelic beings or the divine being of God. It is important to note that the material constituents of living substances and self-moving substances, and even of human spiritual substances (which are embodied), look the same under an electron microscope as merely material nonliving substances, but everyone must admit that they are different. Living substances are fundamentally different from nonliving ones, conscious substances from nonconscious ones, and so forth, even though they look the same under a microscope. An electron microscope cannot detect the power that makes you alive—or the power that makes you conscious—or the transphysical soul that makes you self-conscious and rational.

Now let's return to the Host. Before the consecration that host is a merely material substance. After the consecration, the Host has undergone a huge substantial change. It has moved from a merely material to a living spiritual substance—and much more than that—to a human-divine (hypostatic) spiritual substance. Notice that this huge substantial transformation is undetectable by an electron microscope because the material components of bread (the "accidents") in which the human-divine spiritual substance *appears* still remain the same. However, they are *no longer* the fundamental reality of the Host, which is now a human-divine spiritual substance—the Body, Blood, Soul, and Divinity of Jesus Christ.

Prayer and Fasting

What mercy do I ask from God when I bring my miseries to Him?

Ask the Lord to direct your suffering toward letting go of the things that are still keeping us in our darkness here on earth. We're not in complete darkness, of course, but we're not seeing things clearly because of the darkness we're in. We're looking through a darkened glass,[46] as it were, clouded by inordinate attachments, by ego, by many false desires. We still have a remnant of the seven deadly sins in our hearts.

The first mercy I ask for in my sufferings is "Lord, use this suffering to fill me with more of the Beatitudes and drive out the seven deadly sins." In His wisdom, He is probably not going to do all seven deadly sins or all the Beatitudes at once. But if you ask for the grace, you'll notice that one of the Beatitudes starts to get a little better. At the same time, you start noticing a little more freedom from one of the seven deadly sins. It is a wonderful thing because it is not us, it is God working in us. God is utilizing our suffering to pry us loose from that inordinate attachment so that we can be more and more attached to Him and to His kingdom. That is the first thing that I would ask for.

The second thing I would ask for is the very prayer we see in the Morning Offering, which of course doesn't have to be limited

---

46 1 Cor. 13:12.

to the morning. Just when the suffering happens, do the prayer of St. Thérèse of Lisieux: "Lord Jesus, I join my sufferings to Your sufferings, and I offer them to Your Father for the good of the Church, for the good of salvation, and for the good of the world." That is a prayer that we get also from St. Paul: "Now I rejoice in my sufferings for your sake, and in my flesh I complete what is lacking in Christ's afflictions for the sake of his body, that is, the church."[47] There is nothing ontologically or salvifically lacking in Christ's afflictions. Rather, Jesus made room for us to participate in the order of salvation. So we can offer up our sufferings for the Church, for what we might call for the whole dynamic Kingdom of God coming into being. That includes even the souls in Purgatory, in addition to the people around us who need our prayers. Those are real graces. When you offer your suffering, you must remember that suffering that is offered up is an act of love. It is a gift of self. The Father is going to take your gift and conjoin it to Jesus' own suffering, and then He is going to pour it down onto whomever needs it. But it is not just sufferings; your prayers can achieve that as well.

In the moment of my suffering, I am the one who does the offering, if I remember to offer it. That is a very important thing: we have to remember at the time of suffering to get that offering in, as St. Thérèse was so beautifully aware of and capable of doing.

When I'm asked to pray for someone or something, or when I'm compelled to ask for something, my favorite prayer is the Memorare. I focus on the words of the prayer; I think about the persons who are the subject of the prayer. Is it spontaneous to recite a memorized prayer?

[47] Col. 1:24.

I think absolutely you can memorize a great prayer to use when you're in need. The one thing I was trying to do with the book is to give people a starter set of prayers that was very short, very memorable, very easy to call to mind in order to get the grace going. But if for you the Memorare is so easily called to mind, I would say that is a great prayer. There is a tendency though, during times of fear to have difficulty concentrating on long prayers. Therefore, I would recommend, if the fear is flowing and you're having trouble concentrating on a long prayer—take the first line, or a poignant line, of the prayer and make that your spontaneous prayer and repeat it until your fear level comes down. When it does come down, then say the whole prayer. But the idea behind the spontaneous prayer is that they're so easily repeated. For example, "Thank you!" "Holy Mary, Mother of God, pray for us!" These are so easy to repeat until that fear level comes down—and it will come down because the more you let Mary in, the more you let the Lord in, and so the more the fear level and anxiety level is going to come down. That is the really important thing. It is not just you. It is your connection with God or with Mary, and it is the grace coming from them that is pushing the fear level down. Once your fear level is down, you can just do a Rosary or some other prayer alone or, even better, with someone, and the fear and anxiety level will drop even more. But get the real short, repeatable, memorable ones out in front. There are many of them.

[Doug:] Somebody might claim that it is not really a matter of "grace." You are actually using this as a mantra to calm yourself down. You could use other names and prayers, and you would have had the same relaxing effect. How would you answer this challenge?

It may well be possible that a mantra could calm you down. But speaking for myself, I've only figured out two methods in my whole

life for keeping fear and anxiety under control. The first is spontaneous prayer and the second is to be utterly rational so I can just get
into a frame of mind and be completely cognitive, not concentrating on the feeling of anxiety. I focus on what my backup plan is,
what damage control is needed, and whom do I need to consult.

In my book *The Light Shines on in the Darkness: Transforming Suffering through Faith,* I have a whole chapter entitled "Fear Is Useless:
What Is Needed Is Trust," which is a paraphrase of Jesus' statement
to the synagogue leader whose daughter had died.[48] The main goal
is to get the fear level down. Rationality does work, and more so, the
combination of spontaneous prayers and rationality. But if I *only*
say to myself, "Subconscious mind, let's get some of this fear under
control, holy mackerel!" it will not come under control. If you're
in that situation, it's okay. Be calm. Remember Chief Inspector
Dreyfus, who is being driven mad by Clouseau (Peter Sellers), would
try to control his insanity by repeating, "Every day and in every way,
I'm getting better and better." Eventually, Dreyfus is going to hear
Clouseau's voice and go crazy again.[49] The point is, I am not in
control. Personally, my subconscious is not that strong; it isn't that
controllable; it's not that subject to a mantra. Everybody tells me
I'm the worst guy to try to hypnotize. When the going gets tough,
it is really only prayer that works. The other methods really fail.

*How does fasting relate to prayer? Is one more efficacious than the other,
or do fasting and sacrifice turbocharge prayer?*

That is not a bad way of characterizing fasting: that it turbocharges
prayer. As you probably know, in the Gospel, when Jesus addresses

---

[48] Mark 5:36.
[49] The motion picture *The Revenge of the Pink Panther* (1976).

the fact that the disciples encountered a devil they couldn't cast out, He says, "This kind cannot be driven out by anything but prayer and fasting."[50] Clearly there has to be another dimension of spirituality such that prayers are "turbocharged" in some way. You may ask whether I am saying that, in order for the Lord to hear our prayers, we're going to have to turbocharge them? I'm not saying that at all. I'm saying that the Lord hears our prayers; He judges the prayers that we offer and answers according to His criteria, the most important of which is: Will answering the prayer adversely affect our salvation or the salvation of others we touch or the salvation of others remotely related to us? Most of the time, we don't have nearly enough knowledge of ourselves, others, future contingents, and so much more, so we have to trust God to respond to our prayers as only He can see fit to do.

We can break this down into four criteria that God uses to plan the alleviation of our and others' suffering. First, the Lord will not do anything to undermine even remotely your salvation, and fasting will not influence Him. If there is any remote possibility of answering the prayer as you asked it, the Lord will try to respond in the way that will best give rise to your salvation and the salvation of those you touch.

Second, the Lord will not do anything, even remotely, that will undermine the possibility of salvation of someone else that you might touch or affect. Maybe you don't know that you are going to touch "Joe Doe" in your life, but the Lord knows it, and He sees that the suffering you are going through now is going to touch Joe and his salvation in some future moment. So, God will not alleviate our suffering if it would undermine our salvation or the salvation of family, friends, and other people we influence.

---

[50] Mark 9:29.

Third, He will not alleviate suffering if doing so in some way would undermine our freedom. It is absolutely essential that we remain free. This freedom that we have is awesome, and it is going to determine who we become, whether we're on the wrong road or the right one, even for a horrible tyrant, like Hitler. God would not give Hitler an automatic "lobotomy" because he is going to cause so much trouble. He is going to let Hitler be free because once you start lobotomizing people who are going to cause trouble, where do you draw the line? Like the Parable of the Enemy Who Drops Weeds into the Field of Good Seed, God has to let the two grow up together, and then judge them at their death.

Even though the Lord will allow Hitler to be free, He can simultaneously orchestrate a "divine providential conspiracy" around Hitler so that, ultimately through *our* good efforts and freedom, Hitler will lose the war.

Fourth, God will not alleviate our suffering through a miracle or any other means if it entails undermining somebody else's freedom.

There is one additional important point. God does not see our suffering in isolation from everybody else's. He is looking not just to alleviate *our* suffering, but to find an optimal solution to everyone's suffering that accounts for our paths to salvation, the preservation of our freedom, and of course, our faith, prayers, and fasting.

A quick note on the efficacy of fasting. Fasting can be helpful if you are involved in a spiritual battle, an addiction, or trying to defeat a persistent sin. When we need a force to be present alongside prayer, which is absolutely essential, then fasting can be of great help.

[Doug:] Father, what is it about fasting that helps? Is it because of some type of self-discipline and offering of sacrifice?

It is what I call "prioritization," an establishing of priorities in an area that is manageable, like food or meat on Fridays, something of that nature. If you have established this prioritization to the Lord so that you can ignore something, push it aside, it does help. It builds up as it were, almost like an immunity to poison. It gives us a discipline and resolve to continue prioritizing the Lord over the world around us. And when we have to resist something mightily, if we have the discipline to put aside worldly things in favor of God, it really helps. It's like the athletes' conditioning or the soldiers' boot camp. In this sense, fasting really does turbocharge those spiritual battle kinds of prayers.

Is not spontaneous prayer good prayer at all times? It seems that this would come from a desire for a relationship, for a conversation with God on a constant basis. This seems to be way better than conversation only in various times of trouble.

[Doug:] Isn't it better to be in this ongoing conversation with the Lord, than to be saying these one-off things, circumstantial things?

Let me just put it to you quickly with two conditions. Yes, spontaneous prayer is good all the time. It does make our prayer constant, and, of course, we have been encouraged in Scripture to pray continually. Many saints and Church Fathers endorse and made use of spontaneous prayer. However, you have to be very careful when you say, "continuous prayer" because that doesn't mean that you must constantly be interrupting your workday. For example, if I'm writing, I can't guilt myself into praying continuously in the middle of trying to construct a sentence or a paragraph. If I do this, I'm not going to get any writing done for the Lord. I'm going to be like a manic, going back and forth.

Remember what G. K. Chesterton said about heresy: every heresy is merely an exaggeration of the truth. St. Ignatius knew this very well and put it into his *Spiritual Exercises*. Ignatius knew how the devil operates. He comes appearing as an angel of light. He will give you a pious and good suggestion, even supported by Scripture. But then, he exaggerates it to the point where it disturbs your peace. The devil wants you to give up and despair of having to interrupt everything that you are doing, whether you are working for your family, for the kingdom, or for the good of humanity. So, the devil comes and coaches you to go beyond prudence and says, "No! The more continuous prayer you have, the better! That is what St. Paul means!" Then, you reach the point where you've guilted yourself, and you say, "Oh, I'm a pilot, but I'm not going to concentrate on what is going on in the plane because I need more continuous prayer." Soon you will conclude that this is too much; that you can't keep doing this; that God is expecting too much of you. But that was *not* God. That was your exaggerated application of a scriptural passage *without* the help of the Holy Spirit. It was, in fact, the evil spirit influencing you in order to get you to give up.

It's really a matter of common sense: you can't have your engineers praying continuously as they are running the numbers in preparing to build a bridge because the result could be disastrous. God doesn't want that; only the devil does. But if you do make a mistake, a real critical error, then you're more likely to blame God: "I was praying continuously and look what happened!" But it was not God's advice, it was the evil one's advice that came to you with a pious thought.

Dear Father, I pray every day, mostly the standard prayers Catholics use, like the Rosary and other common prayers. Sometimes I feel that I'm just babbling, even though I try to concentrate and pay attention. Am I really praying, and does God really pay attention?

That is a great question; and the answer is yes! You are really praying. You are consecrating your time to the Lord, and the Lord loves the fact that you are taking time out of your day and spending it with Him, even though sometimes you think that you are rambling. There is no such thing as just rambling. If you are spending time concertedly with the Lord, if you are trying to connect with Him, if you are trying to give Him the praise that is His due, then the Lord loves it. Of course, He loves you anyway, but He loves you in your prayer as well.

Sometimes, instead of thinking that you have to get through the whole Rosary, do this: start off with simply saying these three things to God, "Heavenly Father, I know You are here; I know that You love me; I know that You are guiding me." Then listen because when you say, "I know You are here," you are opening yourself to His presence, so that when you do say a Hail Mary or Our Father after that, it really is going to change that prayer. And if you only do two decades, then good enough because the objective is not necessarily to finish the Rosary. The objective of the prayer is to connect with the Lord, to know His love for you, and to express your love in praise of Him in the midst of knowing His love for you.

Another thing that is really important: sometimes when you are establishing that connection with Him, you notice that when you say, "I know You are guiding me," and then you start listening, something will come up in your mind, and you may think, "*I really didn't think of it.*" For example, for Lent, you realize that you could do something helpful for somebody. Or, you may come to realize that you have been a little impatient of late, and you want to do something about it. You say to yourself, "Oh, I never thought of this before." You may have been thinking about 1 Corinthians 13, and you realized that if love is patient, then God must be unreservedly patient; if love is kind, then God must be unreservedly kind; and if love is merciful, then God must be unreservedly merciful; if love doesn't get angry, then God must be in no way angry. So, you may get an insight. That is what is called "spiritual fruit."

So, sometimes when the insights come to you after you listen to the Lord, when you are getting the spiritual fruit, consider it to be the Lord responding to you. If it is a consolation—an insight about the Lord, or about Scripture, or about something that you could improve on; if it is about something that you never thought of before in the spiritual life, whatever it may be—*stick with it*, as Ignatius says. If there is real consoling spiritual fruit coming from listening, just stick with it. It is okay if you only do one decade; don't get the idea of having to finish because you always do a certain number of prayers. If you do, you risk losing the fruit of the Lord saying that He has something for you; that He is trying to bring some good news or some theological insight. Don't say to the Lord, in effect, "Don't disturb me because I have to finish these eight prayers that I always do!"

[Doug:] Checking off the boxes.

Exactly. "And I'm going to blast through those boxes!"

So, the idea is simply to stick with the fruit. If you only get so far, remember that God is speaking with you and is leading you. If you start getting distractions, move on to the decade.

When I was a novice, one of my distractions was curiosity about how things work. I would look at a boiler and see all of the tubes. I see how that *could* work. There must be boiling water going through the tubes. All of a sudden, I'm thinking, "What does this have to do with prayer?" So, I would move out of the distraction, and back to the Hail Mary—something that kept me going.

The point is to follow the fruit as long as the fruit is there. Then go to your Hail Marys. Then pray that three-part prayer, "Lord Jesus, I know You are here, I know You love me, and I know You are guiding me," and then listen. In this way you are in touch with the Lord, and when you are in touch with the Lord, you come out refreshed. You have been with your best friend, and you become confident in His love. You are consecrating your time to the Lord. Also remember, being consoled in prayer and getting benefits from prayer is entirely a matter of God's grace. We're not giving ourselves grace; we're not manipulating ourselves into feeling consoled, and we're certainly not manipulating God in prayer. Whatever grace is given comes from the Holy Spirit, from the Lord Himself. And when He gives us grace, of course, we thank Him for it. But if it is *not* there, He has something else in mind for us, and so we just keep moving along.

[Doug:] Why do we pray? What relationship does prayer have to our salvation and to our relationship with God?

I would say two things by and large. First, we pray because God wants us to pray. Why does God want us to pray? Because there is grace for us in prayer, and God knows that when we connect with Him, we grow closer to Him and hearts are transformed. We're also going to get that consolation from Him. God is not up there saying, "Hey! I need a little attention here! I want you to pray because I want to know that I'm appreciated." God has nothing to do with Stoic narcissism. He is just the opposite; He is the Father of the Prodigal Son. We can sometimes think that God just wants us to be obsequious and servile and down-on-the-floor humble.

That's not what He wants. What He really wants is to give us the consolation of His companionship. He wants us to be brothers and sisters of Jesus. He wants us to be friends in a relationship with Him, to develop an intimate friendship with Him. And when we do, we are nourished and transformed. We are given over to peace.

This has a lot of good side effects, too, some of which are moral. A close relationship with the Lord in prayer opens the way to moral improvement, such as through growth in the virtues, transformation of our hearts, and a deeper conversion. Alongside moral improvement, we get to be with the Lord in friendship, and with that comes consolation and all of the benefits of friendship. Ask yourself: Why do we want to have friends? It is because friends give us not merely the things that we need for our lives now, like a modicum of security or a modicum of companionship: our friends fill us so we're not empty. We don't want to be lonely. So, when we're in a friendship with God, what I call *cosmic loneliness* disappears. God fills us in a way our human friends could never do: in Him we don't feel that all-consuming emptiness. He fills us with a sense of His home, of His Presence, and of His goodness. Receiving these consolations from the Lord increases in us the theological virtues: faith, hope, and love. That is what really transforms us, and we enjoy being transformed in the process.

Spiritual Discernment

Father, in a recent show you touched on feeling deceived by the devil appearing as an angel of light. At what point can we recognize the devil for who he is? Is it when we're feeling overwhelmed? How do we discern?

St. Ignatius, the founder of the Jesuits, gave a couple of really good pieces of advice in his tract on the "discernment of spirits" in his *Spiritual Exercises*. To make a very long story short: if you are overwhelmed, there might not be a sinister cause; it could be caused naturally or it could be a sign of an angel of light. How do you discern? First, check out possible natural causes: For example, are you under stress? Is there some psychological problem that you are contending with? First make sure the cause is not natural before you try to discern if there is a spiritual cause. Of course, grace does build on nature in many ways, but missing a natural cause as you search for a spiritual cause will not solve your problem.

If there is no natural cause that explains the feeling of being overwhelmed, then consider the first spiritual cause: Am I somehow moving away from God, away from love, away from the Beatitudes? If I'm moving away from Him, I must, as they say, get my act together, which includes Reconciliation and Penance. But if it is not that, then following St. Ignatius, I would look for three signs: the theological virtues—faith, hope, and love. First, are you increasing in trust in God or decreasing? Are you increasing or decreasing in hope in your salvation? Are you increasing or decreasing in your ability to love spontaneously? If your trust in God is waning while you are doing good things and trying to stay on track, and otherwise things are going well, then suddenly you find yourself ready to run for cover and think that God is angry and terrifying, maybe paying you back for something, then you have probably been deceived. St. Ignatius says that in this situation, you have to go back to where you made a decision that led to an erosion of your trust in God. Many things can account for this. Perhaps it began with some things that you started to do or even to believe. Maybe you read a theology book that got you on the wrong track. The bottom line is, if you see your trust in God waning and you entertain the negative notions of God that we just talked about, then beware. That is a real sign that you are being deceived.

Secondly, if you see your hope in your salvation decreasing, particularly if you think that God is completely indifferent to your salvation, then something is wrong! God does not sit up in Heaven debating with Himself, "Spitzer: Heaven or Hell? Hmmm. Heaven or Hell? Hell it is!" That is not the father of the Prodigal Son.[51] Something is amiss. If you have been doing good things, you have been trying to stay on the course of virtue and prayer , and you start thinking horrible things, that is another important sign that you are being deceived.

This can negatively affect otherwise pious thinking. For example, if you start saying to yourself, "If I am in doubt if something is a mortal sin, then it is a mortal sin." I could doubt everything, and if I did, with that view of sin, my life would be a catalog of mortal sins. If my life is a catalog of mortal sins, then I'm for sure going to Hell. So, as a result, you no longer wonder if God is indifferent

---

[51] See the Parable of the Prodigal Son, Luke 15:11–32.

to your salvation, you *"know"* He is against it. At this point, you begin to lose your hope, and you are moving into despair, away from the Holy Spirit. In this state, you are easily overwhelmed because nobody can go on living that way. St. Ignatius says to go back to what you were thinking, what you were deciding, what books you might have been reading, what you started to believe that pulled you off the track, then identify the error or exaggeration in those thoughts and modify them. If you cannot do this for yourself, talk to a priest or spiritual director. Don't persist in the desolation and despair!

When you step back and ask God for guidance, how do you know His will? How do you know when you're getting that guidance?

I would do the following things right up front: Remember the general principle that what is good for your salvation is God's will for you. So the first thing you know is that if you are seeking something that is *not* good for your salvation, then it is not God's will. After prayer and reflection and perhaps conversation with a spiritually mature person, you could figure out what is truly good for your salvation (God's will) and orient yourself toward that. However, we must be careful because we can rationalize things and talk ourselves into apparent goods (which we desire) that are not truly good for our salvation. For example, "Boy, if I went to Harvard, that would be good for my salvation because I'll be better equipped to do so many good things with the powers of articulation that I learn from such good professors." Maybe that would be good for you, but maybe not. Maybe God knows something you don't know. Maybe going to Harvard is, despite what you think, not going to help you toward your salvation. It might be that something like going to St. Thomas University would be better for your salvation.

The first thing you must realize is that God is always looking out for your salvation. Second, you must realize that God is looking out for the salvation of all of the people you touch, and you are going to touch many people over the course of your life, some of whom you don't even know you are touching. The third thing to know is that God is never going to undermine your freedom, and will never undermine the freedom of the people you touch. On the contrary, He is always going to protect your freedom, and in His wisdom He lets human freedom play out, even if in this life the exercise of human freedom causes suffering, which then necessitates the alleviation of your suffering and of others' suffering.

My point is to bring to mind the fact that there are *so many factors* involved in the salvation of one person. God is trying to orchestrate salvation for the entire world with all the innumerable interconnections within it. We can't possibly comprehend all of that: there are too many factors. So, in working out our own salvation, we're going to have to do something else: wait for the Holy Spirit to manifest Himself.

What does this look like? First, the Holy Spirit manifests Himself through the Church. So, learn what the Church teaches and what Jesus is saying in the Gospel. The second requires more explanation. Consider the following scenario, which you may have experienced in some fashion. Someone says something that strikes you as a really important insight. All of a sudden, you are enchanted by this insight, and you start running with it. We call that *inspiration*. Maybe you heard that insight from a friend who you consider to be very wise. Or, you could be watching television and see some political figure who, you think, is stating the truth. He makes some comment, and you say, "There is something important here, something that I need to follow." Maybe you start dreaming about it, and then coincidences happen: you encounter various people or situations that reinforce in you the idea of "a conspiracy of Divine Providence." And all of these coincidences—which are not coincidences—reinforce the idea that you are being led, even inspired. St. Ignatius says that we *still* need to figure this out because this enchantment, this energy that comes interiorly alongside the seeming conspiracy of Providence that reinforces it: How can you be certain whether it is an inspiration from God or from the devil, the latter of whom is always trying to deceive you? St. Ignatius gives us a three-step process based on the three theological virtues of faith, hope, and love.

First, look and see if there is an increase in faith and trust in God in your life. If so, there is a pretty good chance it is from God and that the Holy Spirit is leading you in a godly way. If, on the other hand, you've experienced a decrease in trust, *beware* that you could have been deceived. Likewise, if there is an increase in your hope of salvation, then it probably comes from God. But if there is a decrease in hope, likely not. God only *increases* hope. The evil one, on the other hand, only wants to decrease hope to the point of despair.

Third, is there an increase in the spontaneous ability to love? St. Paul, in 1 Corinthians 13, tells us that that love is patient and kind, never boasts, doesn't rejoice in what is bad, but rejoices in what is good. So if, in following this inspiration, it is easier for you to be patient, kind, and merciful than it is for you to be unkind, boastful, and angry, then it is probably the Holy Spirit leading you. But if you find the opposite, that ever since you started following this inspiration you are more unkind, unmerciful, more proud, more angry, more boastful, then *beware* and put on the brakes. St. Ignatius would say that there is something wrong with that inspiration—that it is not from the Holy Spirit.

So, three steps. When that moment of inspiration, decision, or opportunity arises, and you find it apparently reinforced by the conspiracy of Divine Providence, then *test the spirits*, as St. Paul tells us. If there is an increase in faith, hope, and love, follow it because you are being guided by the Holy Spirit. If you experience a decrease in faith, hope, and love, you must either adjust it in some major way (so that it will increase those three virtues) or abandon it altogether.

In what form does a message from the Holy Spirit come? As an idea, a dream, a spoken message? What type of messages are not from the Holy Spirit?

[Doug:] Obviously, we talked about the negative teardowns not coming from the Holy Spirit. But what about people who receive actual insight from the Holy Spirit?

The short answer is all of the above. Sometimes it could be that somebody just says something in conversation, but what they say galvanizes something within your spirit. You might find what they said not just a curiosity, but fascinating or interesting and something you need to think about more. That could be the voice of the Holy Spirit speaking through that person. But notice how the Holy Spirit galvanizes that sense of faith within your being, that there is some sense, some spiritual truth here—something that you may need to follow.

When I was a college student, I was reading all of the C. S. Lewis books I could get my hands on, and I often found myself saying, "Oh! Wow! That is right!... And, that too!" However, sometimes I would read a book by another author, and have the opposite interior experience. I would have a disconsolate feeling or a sense of doubt or foreboding and confusion. Then I would read about that idea in a Church theology book and discover that what I had read in that other book was wrong. So, there is an intuition with a sense of confidence that can well up in you, and you say, "That is wrong!" Or in the case of C. S. Lewis, "That is right!" Such an inner conviction is frequently a sign of the Holy Spirit. But remember what we said before: you can follow that inner conviction, and most of the time it is going to be the Holy Spirit Who is leading you *if* the inner conviction is accompanied by peace and an increase in faith, hope, and love. Furthermore, if you're trying to follow the teaching of the Church, and you are not rationalizing or trying to talk yourself into something, you are in good shape, particularly if you see, over time, an increase in faith, hope, and love.

[Doug:] How do you discern? Certain people have an intuition that something isn't right, and they don't follow their intuition. I think sometimes we don't trust that as much as we should. We allow ourselves to be convinced by the world, or by others, that we can move past that intuition.

You can, of course, falsely intuit that something is wrong. And don't forget that the devil is trying to deceive you any way he can. The main thing to remember is, if you have an intuition that something is wrong and it's *not* accompanied by accusations, for example, "You little wretch!" or you get that voice of insult: "Who do you think you are? I'm telling you it's fine because I'm the boss," then the intuition is likely correct. But if your intuition that something is wrong is accompanied by telltale signs of the accuser (e.g., insults or demeaning thoughts), then you should be very careful about that moral intuition because it could be the evil one trying to make you scrupulous or to lose hope. Alternatively, if you are getting that insight and it doesn't have any of the signs of the accuser along with it, then you should listen to that inner voice because there probably is something going wrong in your life that needs to be corrected. After you determine that it is wrong, you have to make a plan to correct it in your life.

[Doug:] If you are in a situation like that, what prayer might one use?

If I am discerning something that is wrong, or I get something in a dream, but with that inner conviction that it is right or wrong, I would generally tend to follow the inner conviction. I would pray to the Lord this prayer: "Lord, is this Your will? Lord, give me the wisdom to discern Your will. Lord, give me the light to see whether this is Your will." God will answer, but you have to be very shrewd. Always look for the telltale signs. If that inner conviction and peace are there, and there are not any of the telltale signs of the accuser, who is trying to change your view of God or to portray you as the worm of the Western world—if none of that is present—then, I would say, you are in pretty good shape. But two or three weeks after the fact, test whether your faith, hope and love have increased or decreased. If there is a decrease, you need to make a change.

Suffering and the Love of God

You mentioned in an earlier show that suffering and love are compatible in that they help one another. Could you elaborate on this?

The key is to understand the Christian theological definition of love, particularly what is called *agape* love: *willing the good of the other* (at whatever cost to oneself). Jesus really lays it out, particularly in the Beatitudes.[52] Briefly, "Blessed are the poor in spirit," that is, the humblehearted. "Blessed are the meek," the gentlehearted. "Blessed are those who hunger and thirst for righteousness." Righteousness means readiness for salvation. "Blessed are the merciful." This idea of mercy means forgiveness and also compassion for those who are marginalized. "Blessed are the pure of heart." Purification makes us really authentic people ready for salvation. And then, Jesus declares blessed the peacemakers.

What does all this have to do with suffering? In a word: everything. Suffering is that purgative moment that detaches us from ourselves. I always say that when I'm suffering, I have a hole opened in my heart into which the Holy Spirit can drive a Mack truck full of grace. If you really want to deepen your faith, to deepen your trust in God's providential guidance and care, all have you to do is suffer. That is the best way to do it!

[52] Matt. 5:3–12.

St. Augustine teaches us this principle. Though he was born to a Christian mother (St. Monica), he was, in his own view, quite egotistical. Through a long process—it was ultimately through a variety of different graces, including suffering graces—Augustine began to listen to what he had previously dismissed as valueless: the Holy Scriptures and, particularly, his mother's prayers for him. But for Augustine it was not just his faith, it was a matter of love: "Late have I loved thee, O Beauty so ancient and so new!... Unlovely, I rushed heedlessly among the lovely things thou hast made."[53] Suffering makes us more compassionate if in faith we can open up our hearts. St. Paul in 2 Corinthians 12:7 said that the Lord gave him "a thorn ... in the flesh, a messenger of Satan" to prevent him from getting proud. Whether it was some physical suffering or malady—some people think it was blindness—whatever that was, it literally led to his abandoning himself into the arms of Christ. As Paul's debilitation increased, Christ became stronger within him, so that he wrote to the Corinthians, "When I am weak, then I am strong" (v. 10).

Take note, then, that humble-heartedness and suffering go hand in hand. Gentle-heartedness and suffering go hand in hand because suffering opens us to the goodness of these dispositions, though we naturally tend to shy away from them—particularly, humility. The same holds true for being merciful (forgiving and compassionate), desiring righteousness/holiness, and being a peacemaker. I can attest to this from my own life experience.

When should we begin talking to kids about why God permits suffering? How should we do this?

---

[53] *Confessions*, 10.23.

This may sound cavalier, but how about five years old? Even before I went into kindergarten when I was five years old, there were varieties of suffering that had happened to me. For example, I stuck my hand through a window out of excitement before a swimming lesson, but I didn't have a sense that God was against me. Then, I started going to school and a different kind of suffering began to occur, a reflective suffering. A child in that situation may experience rejection, which is a deeper thing than putting a hand through a window. This can cause a child to ask why it's happening. Such a child is not necessarily asking why about God, but rather why about the suffering. It is at this point that kids begin to question the fairness of life. They are not so much asking why they did something dumb or why they slipped and skinned their knees. That is not a question of fairness, but the question comes out as "Why did God let this happen to me?"

So, I would say that telling children about suffering early in life is good because they will ask questions about the fairness of life, and eventually, apply it to God. There are three Christian ideas or attitudes that we can teach children to help them deal well with suffering.

The first idea concerns God's perspective on suffering—that His foremost desire is to bring us to salvation, and His secondary desire is to alleviate our suffering. The alleviation of suffering may not feel secondary when you are suffering from it, but it is secondary compared to your salvation. Therefore, we must teach children (and adults for that matter) the discipline of asking (in the midst of suffering), "How might God be using this suffering to help me get into Heaven? How can this suffering lead me ever closer to God and to other people?" Even if we can't answer those questions, we have to trust that God is bringing salvation for us and others out of every moment of suffering.

The second idea is that Jesus suffered with us. He did this to help us understand that suffering is inevitable in life and to show us that God will bring salvation out of our suffering as He brought salvation out of His own suffering. People are going to be cruel, and their cruelty is not God's fault. We must teach our children not to blame God for what is not His fault. For example, if somebody makes fun of me on the playground or says something terribly cruel, we cannot blame God for it. God can only do good.

You can, however, ask for God's help. He will help you. You can ask God to let this cruelty be water off the duck's back and that the insult roll right off. Above all, we must ask how God might use this suffering to bring us to salvation—to keep us away from darkness and bring us into the light of His love. But cultivating this attitude takes time and discipline. We need to teach this to our children early on because you can't hide the fact that people can be dark, cruel, and empty; and when they behave this way, they are not representing God; and, therefore, God is not to blame for it. It is also important for adults to show children how they react to adversity, so that children understand these things from adults modeling the right responses.

The third idea is to offer the suffering up to the Lord as Jesus offered His suffering to His Father. One of the most frequently used expressions by my mother was "Offer it up." She was careful to explain that when we offer up our suffering to God, we can use that self-offering to help people in the world—just as Jesus used His self-offering to redeem the whole world. I certainly took this to heart, and when I felt like I was treated cruelly or unfairly, I could always use this to help my parents, my brothers or sisters, or even, as my mother would say, "the poor souls in Purgatory." I felt that suffering had purpose through my self-offering, which took away much of the sting.

[Doug:] Remember pain, sorrow, and suffering are but the kiss of Jesus, a sign that you have come so close to Him that He can kiss you. What do you think about that?

I certainly think this is the case and, speaking for myself, it is principally through suffering that I have made the most progress in my life—in terms of getting out of superficiality and especially with respect to humility, which is so vital in life and for love. If you are not humble, self-sacrifice is pretty much impossible. Yet self-sacrifice is the most noble thing in which we can be involved. So yes, for me, suffering has been a kiss of Jesus.

We have to remember, though, that when the suffering is taking place, we must resist turning inward and getting fearful or anxious. For me, when I was thirty-one years old and studying in Rome, all of a sudden, I was having trouble reading the Hebrew script, which has a minute and detailed system of "pointings" that indicate vowels and other details of the language. I went back to the United States where, after an eye exam, I was told that I would lose my driver's license. Oh no! Losing that was like losing my freedom and autonomy. So, I asked the next important question: How many books can I read before the inevitable happens? I was relieved when they told me that I would still be able to read for another twenty years. Whew! But the fear and the anxiety were real.

In such situations, fear and anxiety are going to come up very naturally. There are ways, though, of dealing with such blows. I have my two little prayers, which I keep talking about: "Thy loving will be done," which I say to the Father; and "Lord Jesus, I place my trust in You." I said these prayers especially when my worsening eyesight was new to me, and I was quite fearful because I *had* to be able to drive and do all the things that I had done before. But if I were not able to drive, what would I do then? What I realized is that I simply had to put myself in the Lord's hands. Once I did that, I found people willing to help me. Suddenly, they came out of the woodwork. Right before my ordination, I literally went into my provincial's office and said, "Tom, I've really got to be honest with you. I have *retinitis pigmentosa*, and my eyes are really going bad, and maybe I only have twenty or thirty years before it's lights out." He asked me what I was thinking, and I said, "If you want me to resign before the ordination … I don't want to be a burden to the whole Society. Just let me go if you think I'm damaged goods and that my value has been seriously compromised." He looked at me and said, "What spirit have you been listening to?" Just like that! Of course it woke me up. God does not make decisions like a utilitarian dictator—the logic that I was using must have come from the evil spirit. God wants to use our suffering and weakness (as we saw in St. Paul—2 Cor. 12:7-10) to bring about our and others' salvation, and to do this, He will help us with a myriad of graces. So, I had to ask for rides to, well, just about everything. I have taught at a number of different places, but I remember especially, when I was teaching at Georgetown, that, if I was not preaching at Holy Trinity Church, I would literally have to ask for rides. Dozens of people would volunteer to give me a ride. I never had to worry about it. And I could always figure out mass transit because I always had enough eyesight to do the reading that I needed to do. Things just really fell into place, and I did begin to trust the Lord, and that trust made a huge difference. Jesus says to the father whose daughter has just died, "Fear is useless. What is needed is trust."[54]

That is, in fact, the case when suffering comes. Fear is use-less. Anxiety is one of the most debilitating things. Give it over

[54] Mark 5:36.

to Jesus and start looking for the *opportunities* of suffering. It will make a huge difference. There are many opportunities to change your life's path, to get out of the superficial and into deeper faith, prayer, humility, and compassion. Mother Angelica used to say, "Sometimes, my worst day of pain and suffering is my best day in God's eyes, if I have borne it cheerfully."

The Christian and the World

In It but Not of It

Father, how do we live in the world and not be part of it? How do we live that transcendent happiness while we must still be in the world to earn a living?

When I was president of Gonzaga University, I had to be competent in order to do the job well. How did I have such competency? I tried to develop myself, develop my education, develop my speaking abilities, my analytical abilities, my quantitative abilities, and my judgment. We all have a responsibility to develop those things, those so-called "level-two characteristics" in our lives. All of these things are good and will be useful. However, we don't live for them. What I mean by "live for them" is we don't live to be better than other people, or smarter than somebody else so that we can point to our accomplishments. If that is our motivation, then get ready for disappointment. Rather, I want to cultivate my intelligence so I can do good for the Lord, for the students I teach, and the communities I serve. Most importantly, I want to develop my integrity before God.

[Doug:] Back in the 1980s they used to say, "He who dies with the most toys wins." Remember that bumper sticker? It was very popular in its time.

It is pathetic, really; a complete underestimation of human intellect, ability, spiritual and moral judgment, and just about everything else.

Challenges to Faith

Father, how do you continue to hold onto your faith when the culture tells you that you are wrong or in the minority? Because of this, the faithful often suffer in loneliness. One of the things that you mentioned on your website—one of the root causes of the decline of faith among young people—is the perceived conflict between suffering and love. This affects a lot of people today.

I might break it down into a couple of different categories. When people challenge my faith, my first reaction is to return the challenge with the question, "What is the cause of your *not* believing in God?" Is it because you think that science contradicts God? If so, then you should know that 51 percent of scientists do profess belief in God or a spiritual reality (41 percent are agnostics and atheists), and 66 percent of young scientists profess belief in God or a spiritual reality.[55] At least half of those who do not profess belief are agnostics. So, only a minority of scientists (21 percent overall and 14 percent of young scientists) are atheists. Why? Because there is considerable scientific evidence for an intelligent Creator from contemporary cosmology and evidence for life after death from peer-reviewed medical studies of near-death experiences and terminal lucidity.

If you want to see this scientific evidence for God, please go to my website, magiscenter.com. The site is for everybody; and especially in the case where you aren't able to answer a person's question, you can lead them to the site where they will find free articles and videos that detail the evidence for God in contemporary physics. There is an enormous amount of evidence: of a beginning,

---

[55] See "Scientists and Belief," Pew Research Center, November 5, 2009, https://www.pewforum.org/2009/11/05/scientists-and-belief/.

of fine-tuning for life in the initial constants and conditions of our universe, and much more.

When answering these challenges, it is helpful to try to get a fix on what is moving the person confronting you to challenge the Faith. Sometimes it is personal suffering in their lives, and on that topic, I've written a book, *The Light Shines on in the Darkness: Transforming Suffering through Faith*. In chapter 7, I talk about "the opportunities of suffering." I think that Christians ought to photocopy that chapter. Who cares about the money! Copy the chapter and take them through the opportunities, because I think that so many people waste time resenting sufferings instead of seizing the opportunity and the graces that are found in them. As Christians, we need to help people recognize the opportunities of suffering—particularly in developing faith and love.

Perhaps unbelief is not a result of science or suffering. Maybe it is the perception that religion has caused a lot of suffering: wars and terrorism in the name of religion. There is some truth in this concern, but I think we have to point out the many more good things religion has done throughout the centuries. Religious people have allowed themselves to be adversely caricatured and, unfortunately, many don't fight back. We need to say, "Hey, just a cotton-pickin' minute, here. You know, before Christianity, what did you have in the Roman Empire that was of any worth in terms of public welfare? *Nothing.* It was Christianity that started public welfare and now—surprise!—the Catholic Church is the largest of all public welfare systems in the world. Where was good ole Rome in public education? *Nowhere.* Then all of a sudden, after Christianity came on the scene, there is extensive public education, and it is the Catholic Church that operates the largest education system in the world today. And where was good ole Rome on the public health scene and in founding hospitals to care for the sick?

Again, *nowhere*. Essentially, it was the Christians that got the public health system going. It's no surprise that the Catholic Church operates the largest international healthcare system in the world today, overseeing over 26 percent of all world healthcare."

"And hey! Where was good ole Rome on the issue of slavery?" Slaves were on the lowest rung of existence, constituting about 35 percent of the Roman population. It was Christianity that broke down slavery by not only advocating for them, but also providing them with education, welfare, and healthcare, thereby giving them status, despite what the Empire was doing to deprive them of a humane existence. So, let's just take a look at some good things about religion before we get pegged with the Crusades again.

There is an article at magiscenter.com that details everything that I've alluded to just now: what is the teaching of Jesus, and what has the Church done from the early centuries all the way until today. Take a look at that article.[56]

[Doug:] I understand what you are saying, and probably most of the audience agrees with you, but outside of this "bubble" people think that it is natural for people to do good. It is the structures that make them do bad things. Is it just intrinsic to us to do the right thing? What do you say to that?

This is such a romantic ideal: the virtuous natural man, following Rousseau. On the other side of the same coin, you have Machiavelli saying that human beings are rotten to the core, and the only way you control that rotten impulse is through the Prince, the despot who comes down with force and terror to make people virtuous despite themselves. These two alternatives have kept right on going:

---

[56] Go to MagisCenter.com.

some people line up with Rousseau and some with Machiavelli. However, reality shows that most of us fall somewhere in between—a little bit of natural virtue and a little bit of rottenness—the percentages differ widely among different people. My opinion is that our "rottenness" comes mostly from pride and narcissism. Think about it: shortly after Adam and Eve were created with free agency, the devil enters the picture and tells them, "You can be gods, too!" Really? Only a little deception, and we're off and running! The effects last to this very day. Nevertheless, the Church has always held that even after the Fall, human beings were essentially good. We didn't go the Calvinistic extreme of the "total depravity" of human beings. However, the Church holds that there is a significant darkening of heart and need for redemption. If we don't find a way to get that redemption, both through the teaching of Jesus and through the grace of the Holy Spirit working through the Church—the Holy Spirit working in our hearts—if all we have is our own free will to get us to follow Christ's teaching, then I think it will be very difficult to resist the darkness. Yes—other religions can reinforce moral teaching, faith, worship, and prayer, which, in turn, help us overcome the darkness, but Christ's teaching, Spirit, and Church are the most direct and comprehensive means to resist that darkness.

Abortion and Contraception

Science has proven that the human embryo is physically alive. We know that a child's heart can be seen circulating blood in just twenty-two days after conception. Scientifically and soundly, how else can we argue that life begins at conception?

[Doug:] So, certainly now, with the ultrasound, we can see and hear a lot of things we couldn't before.

I don't think there is even a question, scientifically, that a full human being is present at fertilization. We know this from DNA sequencing, which goes all the way back to roughly 1978, that the full human genome is present in the single-celled zygote. Dr. Jérôme Lejeune testified to this in two appellate court decisions, and it is accepted by well over 96 percent of the international professional biological community today. Furthermore, it is unquestionable that mitochondrial DNA (which identifies us specifically as human by the genetic contribution of humanity's common mother) is present in the zygote, and it is unquestionable that the totipotent single-celled zygote is metabolizing and living, and it is unquestionable that this one cell will give rise to every cell in a person's body throughout the entire course of his or her life. Hence, this single-celled zygote and its complete human genome is a living, *substantially whole*, unique human being. This means that nothing of human substance will be added to that unique human being throughout the course of his or her existence. Yes—there will be nutriment and other *non*-substantial contributions made to this human being, but that single-celled zygote has everything that will make it uniquely human and humanly unique throughout his or her lifetime.

It should be noted that the vast majority of professional biologists believe that a new unique human being comes into existence at *fertilization*. An international survey of 5,577 biologists showed that 96 *percent* (5,354) of them affirmed that fertilization is the origin of a new, unique, specifically human being.[57] If most biologists

[57] Lynn D. Dowd "Brief of Biologist as Amici Curiae in Support of Neither Party: Thomas E. Dobbs v. Jackson Women's Health Organization," July 29, 2021, submitted to the United States Court of Appeals for the Fifth Court as well as United States Supreme Court, https://www.supremecourt.gov/DocketPDF/19/19-1392/185254 /20210729125335060_19-1392%20Dobbs%20v.%20JWHO%20

and physicians agree that a new, unique, substantially whole human being exists at fertilization, why would we not recognize the inalienable rights to life, liberty, and the pursuit of happiness of this substantially whole, unique human being? If we want to make a gratuitous exception for pre-born human beings on the basis of subjective preference, what is to prevent future legislatures and courts from refusing to recognize the inalienable rights of other substantially whole, unique human beings? Should we alienate the inalienable from the physically challenged, the mentally challenged, the emotionally challenged, the economically challenged, the elderly? The question is not only "Where should we stop this?" but also "How are we going to stop this when we have eliminated the criterion upon which our Declaration of Independence bases inalienable rights—they belong by nature to *all* human beings?"

The problem arose from the Supreme Court's majority in *Roe v. Wade*, where the Court made a most specious distinction between human beings and persons. In the majority opinion, the Court acknowledged that the appellant's case would collapse if human personhood could be established. In fact, the appellant and her lawyers had so much as agreed to the fact. Then, stunningly, the Court made this distinction and said that they could not establish the personhood of this substantially whole human being. They made this distinction because some experts they had consulted were unsure about the human status of the fetus. If they had waited four years, they would have known that a single-celled zygote was a substantially whole human being. Four years later, science knew that there is mitochondrial DNA present in a single-celled zygote as

---

Amicus%20Brief%20of%20American%20Center%20for%20 Law%20and%20Justice%20and%20Bioethics%20Defense %20Fund.pdf.

well as a full and unique human genome, and that the single-celled zygote will generate and be the unity of every cell in that human being's body throughout their lifetime. So four years later, science knew that a new unique, substantially whole human being exists at fertilization. Since personhood means that the fetus is deserving of protection under the law, the unwarranted denial of personhood to these unique, substantially whole human beings resulted in the Court sanctioning the killing of those unique, substantially whole human beings based on the Court's *ignorance* of evidence — *not* on the *presence* of incontrovertible scientific evidence. If the Court had waited until science could make a determination, they could not have legitimately sanctioned the killing of millions of innocent human beings on the basis of their specious and unwarranted distinction between "human being" and "person." The humanity of the single-celled zygote would have been established, and personhood would have to have been accorded on the basis of universal justice. This was not just a fatal flaw, but also an immeasurable tragedy and an egregious violation of justice.

How did they get away with this specious distinction that cancelled the inalienable rights of unique, substantially whole human beings? They argue from silence to the denial of inalienable rights. The only time we ever see this illogical and flawed argument in the U.S. is in the sanctioning of slavery, particularly in the Dred Scott decision where the Supreme Court unanimously held, on the basis of silence in the Constitution, that "Negros" did not have the right to liberty and should be subjugated to the "superior race." In *Roe v. Wade*, the Court made a similar argument, saying that they were uncertain about personhood of the unborn because some experts were uncertain, and they looked at the language of the Fourteenth Amendment and failed to find that prenatal personhood was established. What does that mean? It means that the

Fourteenth Amendment is silent on the personhood of prenatal living, substantially whole human beings with a unique, full human genome. Now, there is a very important dictum in the law that "silence means silence." In other words, you cannot construe silence to mean "Yes" or "No." So, it is always unjust to interpret silence as meaning one or the other. This is a well-known dictum, and the Court abrogated it. As a consequence, the Court said because they found no specific mention of prenatal personhood in the Fourteenth Amendment, such personhood doesn't exist, and it is okay to kill that fetus. This is an egregious violation of Logic 101, as well as Legal Evidence 101 and Morality 101.

When you further analyze what the Court has done, you find that they have completely reversed the entire logic of our constitutional system. Instead of saying a unique, substantially whole human being should be considered a person until proven otherwise, the Court held that a substantially whole human being should *not* be considered a person (deserving of protection under the law) until proven to be a person. But this gets us into the problem of who gets to define "person" if personhood does not belong to *every* unique, substantially whole human being by their very nature. Evidently, the Court has appropriated unto itself the power to abrogate the inalienable rights of every human being and to sanction the killing of any human being whom it does not consider to be a person—or cannot be proved to be a person according to its subjective declaration.

We see similar reasoning in the Dred Scott decision where the Court declared that it was not up to them to prove that black human beings should not be considered protected by the law from unjust and unnecessary harm. Instead, they said that the Court is only responsible for proving that black people should be considered citizens, and the Consitution is silent on this. So, the country can enslave them.

In both the *Roe v. Wade* and Dred Scott decisions we are reminded of St. Augustine's dictum, "An unjust law is no law at all!"[58] Can anyone deny that forcing a unique, substantially whole human being to prove they are a person (according to a court's subjective standard) before granting them the fundamental rights to life and liberty is wholly unjust, and as such, should not be considered a law of any merit deserving of respect by the populace? Clearly, the Court chose not to honor the true intention of the Founding Fathers, the common law, and the principles elucidated by Francisco Suárez, Hugo Grotius, John Locke, and Thomas Jefferson. These pillars of legal and political thought would be appalled at the complete abrogation of natural rights. They would have recognized the errors and inhumanness in distinguishing "human being" from "human person," and placing the burden of proof on demonstrating that someone who is a substantially whole human being is a person. The Supreme Court, in *Roe v. Wade*, has gotten away with this denial of inalienable rights and the reversal of our constitutional priorities because it was politically expedient. This has resulted in a specious decision, an inhumane and unjustifiable precedent, which today, even after the reversal of Roe in *Dobbs v. Jackson Women's Health Organization*, is being perpetuated by state laws that allow even greater deprivation of inalienable rights of the preborn.

More than 1.43 billion babies worldwide since 1980 have been aborted. What happens to all these innocent, immortal souls that only have the "stain of Original Sin"? Can they ever get to Heaven? Can they be purified in Purgatory? After all, their most fundamental right was taken away.

---

[58] St. Augustine, *On the Free Use of the Will*, bk. 1, sect. V.

Those little children are in Heaven, no question about it, though they have the stain of Original Sin. It was previously thought that maybe they were put into a separate place called limbo[59] because they had not been baptized. Though limbo was never a dogmatic teaching of the Church, the Second Vatican Council formally rescinded it. The Church now entrusts such infants to the mercy of God, Who desires that all be saved. As for aborted children, because they are innocent, because they were killed unjustly, we believe they would have the same status as the Holy Innocents, who were slaughtered because of the arrival of Jesus. We believe that every last one of them is with the Lord in Heaven. They too are expressing the fullness of who they would have become because their souls are fully human souls. Are they going to be allowed to develop in some way? Though the Church does not say how that occurs, or whether they experience some sort of childhood in Heaven, studies of near-death experiences indicate that they do experience childhood in Heaven.[60] We know that all of them will be brought into the heavenly kingdom. That, of course, doesn't excuse us from the moral and ethical obligation to protect those human lives. They deserve to be treated as God intended—to have the possibility of a biological life with parents and family, and not to be put to death.

---

[59] Limbo was hypothesized in the Middle Ages as a solution to the problem of infants who die unbaptized. Because of the lack of Baptism, they didn't merit the Beatific Vision, but because they had no personal sin, they didn't merit punishment, either. In essence, limbo was conceived of as a perfect natural existence.

[60] See J. Steve Miller, *Is Christianity Compatible with Death Bed and Near-Death Experiences*, vol. 3 (n.p.: Wisdom Creek Press, 2023), 42, 109, 171, 180-181, 334. See also Todd Burpo, *Heaven Is for Real* (Nashville: Thomas Nelson, 2011).

In sum, God does, in His unconditionally loving mercy, take these innocent preborn children to Himself. It is interesting to note that of the little children who have near-death experiences—who undergo clinical death, for example, via drowning or heart attack or something of that nature—a large majority have a very positive near-death experience, and only a small percentage cannot remember that anything happened to them. It is just the reverse for adults: 80 percent of adults don't remember anything after clinical death; just 20 percent have a positive near-death experience. We do know that God very much cares about children, not just because of their near-death experiences, but because of Jesus' own declaration: "See that you do not despise one of these little ones; for I tell you that in heaven their angels always behold the face of my Father who is in heaven."[61]

[Doug:] Let me ask you this, since you touched on it. Some make a religious argument for abortion. As Father said, since these children end up going to Heaven anyway, it is actually a wonderful eternal outcome for them. And so this young lady gets to avoid having to deal with what she has done. Why is that a bad outcome?

Well, it's morally bankrupt. We are responsible as human beings to a code of just ethical behavior. The very minimum that we're expected to do is to follow what is called "the Silver Rule." You've no doubt heard of "the Golden Rule," which is a high ethical standard. The Silver Rule is the minimum ethical standard expected of every human being, and it's written into the conscience of every human being. "Do not do unto others what you would not have them do unto you." In other words, if harm to another human

---

[61] Matt. 18:10; see also Matt. 19:14.

being is avoidable, then you must avoid it. For example, you are in an automobile, and you can't stop it in time to avoid an accident. If a harm is unavoidable, then you must minimize it. Don't do unnecessary harm. If you are not going to abide by that, then life will become ugly, brutish, and short.

My shorthand way of looking at this minimum justice (minimal ethical commitment) is, if you have a friend who says, "I really need to do unnecessary harm to people in order to be fulfilled in life—or I just need to kill some of my children in order to be fulfilled in life," then avoid that person at all costs. They have rejected the principle of justice, intrinsic dignity, inalienable rights, and personal responsibility before God. And they certainly deny the dictates of their conscience. Psychiatrists would call that sociopathy. There is a distinction between *malum in se* ("evil in itself") and *malum prohibitum* ("evil because prohibited by law"). We all have a deep sense in our conscience of what is evil in itself—fundamentally unnecessary and unjust deeds that do significant harm to others (e.g., murder or malicious lies or depriving people of the necessities of life, etc.). For this reason, crimes which are *malum in se* cannot be excused by ignorance—and therefore, ignorance cannot excuse violating this law. On the other hand, crimes which are *malum prohibitum* are not known in our conscience. They must be learned within a particular culture or polity in which they are prohibited. Hence, ignorance is an excuse for violating these kinds of laws.

Now here's the point—abortion objectively is the killing of a unique, substantially whole human being (which can be established scientifically). Moreover, this unique, substantially whole human being is innocent. Since such a killing of an innocent human being always objectively can be avoided (it is unnecessary), it is the grossest violation of minimum justice. As such, it is *malum in se* (evil in itself), and unless one is a sociopath, everyone should be expected to know that this is objectively wrong. In answer to your question then, the young lady should not kill her child because it is one of the grossest violations of minimum justice and the standards according to which we all must live, lest our lives within this society become brutish, ugly, and short—violence begetting violence without the shield of justice.

[Doug:] Is that the reason why there is so much anger attached to this issue for some people?

Yes. I think sometimes, when you see a lot of moral indignation and outrage toward something that is completely unethical and wrong, for example, indignation of pro-life people toward pro-abortion people, there is anger there because the pro-lifers do strongly believe that people *should* know that a baby's being in utero doesn't give license to kill it anymore than it gives an excuse to kill the same baby outside the womb. Partial-birth abortion, in particular, is so brutal that it provokes great outrage. People ask in disbelief, "How can this be excused? This is clearly a case of an unjustifiable, unnecessary harm, namely, the taking of another human life. How can you possibly justify this under any circumstance? Simply because part of the baby's body is still in utero? It makes no sense." And so, of course, we do get outraged, and justifiably so, but we've got to calm down so that we can rationally explain why it is wrong. Our culture has literally planted a seed, giving legal sanction and justification for this crime.

Here is the basic logic: if something becomes legal, it becomes normal; and if it becomes normal, it becomes moral. Why? Because if you give something legal sanction, then people start doing it, mistaking legal sanction for moral sanction; and of course, if they start doing the deed in great numbers, which they have in the case of abortion, then it seems to be moral because everybody is doing it. Now that the horses are out of the barn, merely reversing the legal sanction will be ineffective for turning the issue around because people are already convinced that it is not only moral, but also their right to kill a preborn human being. We will have to, therefore, start educating in our schools about the immorality of what seems to be completely obvious—killing human beings, whether in the womb or not, is wrong. By the way, this point can be proven without recourse to religion. Today, we can scientifically establish on the basis of genomic evidence and the unique characteristics of the human zygote, that a single-celled zygote is a substantially whole human being. With this established, we need only show that the unnecessary killing of this innocent human being is a gross injustice by any standard. If we don't make use of the scientific evidence and rational arguments, we are left only with screaming matches that go nowhere.

[Doug:] Is that a problem unique to the American mindset? Or is that something that we share with other cultures around the world?

I think it is very normal in Western culture and certainly in some Asian cultures—and certainly in the United States, where the law is so highly respected. Remember, in our American culture, the law is identified with justice. By the way, that identification is largely based on the ideas of St. Augustine, who penned the famous dictum, "It seems to me that a law that is not just, is not a law at all." What Augustine was saying is that every positive law—a law passed by a legislature or one that becomes a law by judicial action or precedent—must always correspond to the higher principle of justice, which requires us to give every human being their due and not to cause any human being an unnecessary harm. This is minimal justice. The whole idea of justice being higher than the law was taken into the European legal world, and so the law was enshrined with dignity: think of the Statue of Liberty; or in Washington, D.C., in front of the Supreme Court building, the statue of Justice herself, blindfolded with the scales, indicating that impartial justice is the guiding principle of law. A noble thing indeed, and of course, I agree that justice is noble. It moves my heart. St. Augustine regarded justice the same way, but he recognized that if a "law" does not follow justice—that is to say, that if it abrogates the principle of no unnecessary harm (non-maleficence) and of giving each person their due—then it is no law at all.

As you probably know, this principle has been used repeatedly in acts of civil disobedience. It certainly was quoted by Thomas Jefferson, by Martin Luther King in his "Letter from Birmingham Jail," and by Gandhi. So we give to the law a powerful moral force within our culture because we believe that it is commensurate and consistent with justice; but in point of fact, in the case of abortion, it is not, because abortion is the unnecessary killing of an innocent person (which can be shown scientifically to be a unique, substantially whole human being). Now, if this law is a gross violation of justice, then that law, according to Augustine, is no law at all. It is a mere pretense to legitimate law—and the people who passed that law have abdicated their responsibility to maintain justice in the law and to prevent the arbitrary passage of unjust laws in order to please certain interest groups with influence and funds. These legislators and judges have a duty not only to justice itself, but also to the people of the United States, and especially to the innocents who will be harmed by this abrogation of justice.

[Doug:] Isn't that on one level what the Nuremberg trials were about? Those on trial said, "I was just following orders," the classic concentration camp excuse. But there is a higher law that supersedes this situation.

Exactly. This is what we're following in the United States.

I don't see how abortion can be completely eradicated as long as artificial birth control is the order of the day. Abortion is built on the mentality of demand for artificial birth control.

[Doug:] Artificial birth control gives you the autonomy to be able to say, "I'm in control of my own body; I'm in control of how these things work." To some degree, abortion is the ultimate version of birth control.

Certainly there is a linkage between people's thinking about artificial birth control and about abortion. However, when we deal with the ethical issue, we have to distinguish between the two acts because they are morally very different. To block conception is one thing. To perform or undergo an abortion, even if on just a single-celled zygote, is to kill a substantially whole human being. It doesn't matter the method: it could be the morning-after pill, or it could be RU-486, or any abortifacient. The same holds true for any other intervention to kill an already formed fetus, single-celled zygote. Now I'm not saying contraception isn't serious. It *is*. What I'm saying is that abortion is really, really serious, and we don't want to make our ethical argument against abortion dependent upon the argument against artificial contraception. We must keep the two separate. But yes, in our own mind, looking at the pedagogical side of things, the mentality of artificial birth control leads to abortion, and the person who moves from the lesser to the greater here crosses a huge threshold when they start the killing activity that is the killing of an innocent human being.

[Doug:] Some make the case that some contraceptives are abortifacients already and in some cases they have crossed over already.

An abortifacient is not a contraceptive, because it does not block conception. It is the killing of a substantially whole human being.

Father, the biggest hurdle to overcome in putting an end to abortion seems to be softening the human heart. How do we reconcile change in the hearts of men and women? What loving steps should we take in transforming our neighbors' hearts so that they choose life?

[Doug:] Also, sometimes we can get ourselves so focused on the argument, discussion, and the tussle, that we forget that we do need to change peoples hearts at the same time.

I'm going to recommend a book because this is a big question. In my book *Ten Universal Principles*, at the end with the tenth principle, I talk about the four levels of happiness. I think there are a lot of really good human beings out there who would respond to moving from level two to levels three and four. I'm going to give a very brief explanation and talk about the consequences of helping people to make that move because I think you are right: a softening of the heart is what is required.

We can do this through a logic of contribution and faith. Let's consider the four levels. Level one means that I am finding my happiness and my meaning in life by means of physical stimulation and material well-being. So, having a Mercedes with leather upholstery, or getting lots of ice cream cones and bowls of linguine, that is what is really going to make a meaningful and happy life for me. The second level—and there are many people on that level in our culture—is ego-comparative happiness. People on that level say, "As long as I have more success, more intelligence, more promotions, more power, more control, more achievements than other people, or I'm just in that top 20 percent, I'm going to be happy and have a meaningful life. But if not, I'm going to be unhappy." The problem with this level is that it really does push us into ego-comparative problems, such as jealousy, fear of failure, meaninglessness, and so on.

The third level is the contributive view of happiness. It can best be described by the word *love*. Instead of wanting to be better than everybody (level two) or have more creature comforts (level one), we decide to make optimal positive contributions to somebody or to something beyond ourselves. That is, we make an optimal contribution to our families, our friends, our church, the Kingdom of God, the society, our workplace, our colleagues, and so forth. We decide that we're really going to predicate our lives on making an optimal positive difference to others rather than trying to be better than them or more successful than them.

The fourth level of happiness, as you might have guessed, would be faith. We're spiritual beings; we desire the transcendentals: perfect love, beauty, truth, and goodness. We want to be perfect, meaning in harmony with God. I don't know if you are familiar with Dr. Carolyn Weber, a former strident atheist who became a Christian while at Oxford.[62] Before her conversion, she struggled with emptiness, loneliness, fear, feelings of inadequacy, and guilt. Essentially, she was so lonely for God that when she finally submitted to Him and accepted Him, she discovered that God not only exists but that He is self-giving Love. My point is that we have this extreme need for a transcendental life in faith and harmony and communion with God.

There are techniques explained in my books (*Ten Universal Principles* and *The Four Levels of Happiness*) to be used to get out of

---

[62] Dr. Carolyn Weber, *Surprised by Oxford* (Nashville: Thomas Nelson, 2011).

level one and level two. There are also techniques in the books to describe how people are looking at life and others, and to help move them from levels one and two to levels three and four. If they do this, everything in the books about levels three and four (contributive and faith based/transcendent happiness) become so much more apparent. For those who move from levels one and two to levels three and four, it will be just like it was for Carolyn Weber. She had a change of heart and realized her need for God, church, and to follow the love revealed by God. With this disposition of heart, the pro-life position becomes virtually self-evident. Authentically illumined by the love of God, no one can say that intentionally killing an innocent preborn baby is morally or even naturally good, let alone the will of God. Abortion is revealed in its true absence of light, the antithesis of good, and the will of the evil spirit, who has used every kind of sophistry and vice to turn light into darkness.

About the Author

Rev. Robert J. Spitzer, S.J., Ph.D., is the founder and president of the Magis Center. A scholar, teacher, author, and seasoned leader, Spitzer is a preeminent theologian and philosopher, specializing in the philosophy of science. His other areas of expertise are ethics and leadership. As president of Gonzaga University from 1998 to 2009, he significantly increased the university's programs in faith, ethics, service, and leadership as well as the enrollment, endowment, and facilities. Spitzer has made many TV appearances, including *Larry King Live* (discussing the origins of the universe with Stephen Hawking and Deepak Chopra), *The Today Show*, the History Channel's *God and the Universe*, and the PBS series *Closer to the Truth*. He has a weekly television program on EWTN—*Father Spitzer's Universe*—and is the author of eighteen books and many scholarly articles.